THE
Leadership
Transition
Guide

Whole Human Leadership in Your First 90 Days

Victoria Pelletier

UNSTOPPABLE YOU LLC

www.victoria-pelletier.com

Published by Unstoppable You LLC
ISBN: 979-8-9896797-6-8 (Paperback)
ISBN: 979-8-9896797-7-5 (Digital/eBook)
First Edition, 2026

The stories and examples in this book are drawn from the author's professional experience. Where individuals are referenced by first name only, names have been changed to protect privacy.

The information in this book is intended for educational and professional development purposes. It does not constitute legal, financial, or therapeutic advice.

www.victoria-pelletier.com

THE LEADERSHIP TRANSITION GUIDE

Whole Human Leadership in Your First 90 Days

WHAT'S INCLUDED IN EVERY SECTION

Narrative & frameworks grounded in Whole Human Leadership and 30+ years of real experience | **Story anchors** from Victoria's career | **Self-assessments, templates & action planning tools** to complete in real time

THE FIRST 90 DAYS ARE NOT WHAT ANYONE TELLS YOU THEY ARE

I have done this more times than I can count on both hands.

Walked into a new organization — or a newly acquired one, or a restructured one, or one that had been promised a fresh start and was quietly terrified of what that meant — and spent the first week figuring out where the bodies were buried while trying to look like I already knew.

The first time I did it, I was 24. COO. New mother. Youngest executive in the building by almost two decades, and the only woman at the table. The role was a significant stretch, and everyone in the organization knew it, including me. I had been brought in because I was good — genuinely good — and because I had earned it. None of that made the first 90 days any less disorienting.

Since then, I have stepped into new roles, new mandates, and new organizations more times than most leaders do in an entire career. I have navigated over 40 mergers and acquisitions — which means I have had the particular joy of entering businesses mid-transformation, mid-panic, and mid-identity crisis more times than I'd care to admit. I have inherited teams that were thriving and teams that were unravelling. I have walked into cultures that were genuinely healthy and cultures that were performing well while quietly disintegrating. I have sat in the first all-hands meeting as the new leader and watched 200 people try to decide, in real time, whether I was worth following.

I know what the first 90 days actually feel like from the inside. Not the polished version. The real one.

And I know what it costs when leaders get them wrong.

> **I have navigated over 40 mergers and acquisitions. I know what the first 90 days actually feel like from the inside. Not the polished version. The real one.**

What Goes Wrong — and Why

The most common mistake I see new leaders make is not a strategic error or a tactical misstep. It is a posture problem. They arrive in the role trying to prove something — to justify the hire, to demonstrate that the confidence placed in them was warranted, to signal that they have the answers. And in doing so, they skip the one thing that would have made everything else possible: genuinely understanding what they have stepped into before they start changing it.

The second most common mistake — and this one I have made myself — is treating the first 90 days as purely operational. Learn the business, map the stakeholders, build the plan. All necessary. None sufficient. Because the most important things you need to understand in a new role are not in any briefing document. They are in the room. They are in the silences. They are in the Unseen Employees that nobody is sending you to meet. They are in the cultural dynamics that will determine whether your strategy gets executed or quietly strangled.

And the third mistake — the one that derails leaders who are otherwise genuinely capable — is failing to bring their whole self to the role. Arriving in armour. Keeping the personal at the door. Performing the kind of leader they think this organization needs rather than being the kind of leader their team actually requires. I was guilty of this one too, for longer than I'd like to admit. It earned me a nickname I will tell you about shortly.

There is a better way. That is what this guide is.

Why I Wrote This — and Why It's Different

I have spent over 30 years in corporate leadership. I have led businesses through crisis, transformation, and growth across three continents. I have coached and mentored hundreds of leaders at every level — from first-time managers stepping into their first team to C-suite executives inheriting organizations that needed to be fundamentally rebuilt.

In that time, I have read most of the leadership transition literature. There are excellent frameworks out there — Michael Watkins' The First 90 Days is a genuine classic and worth your time for its analytical rigor. But most of what exists in this space is strong on operational strategy and thin on the human dimension. Strong on what to do, and quiet about who to be while you're doing it.

This guide fills that gap.

The Leadership Transition Guide is built on two frameworks I have developed over a career of doing this the hard way. The first is Whole Human Leadership — my philosophy that the most effective leaders are not the ones who leave their humanity at the door, but the ones who bring all of it deliberately and strategically to work. The second is the personal brand framework from my book, Influence Unleashed — because who you are and how you show up is as important as what you know and what you decide.

Every section is grounded in real experience — my own and that of the leaders I have worked with, coached, and occasionally had to have very difficult conversations with. The stories are real. The frameworks have been tested in conditions that were not academic. The tools are the ones I wish someone had handed me in those first overwhelmed weeks at 24, standing at the head of a table, wondering what came next.

> **Most leadership transition literature is strong on what to do, and quiet about who to be while you're doing it. This guide fills that gap.**

What This Guide Is — and What It Isn't

This is not a checklist. It is not a generic onboarding program. It is not a collection of best practices assembled from the latest research on leadership transitions, though it draws on that research where it is relevant and properly attributed.

This is a guide for leaders who want to do it right — who understand that the first 90 days are not just a probationary period to survive but a foundational window to build something that lasts. Something that your team will still be talking about, in the best possible way, long after you have moved on to whatever comes next.

It will ask things of you that most leadership guides don't. It will ask you to be honest about your own default patterns under pressure. It will ask you to go looking for the people nobody is sending you to meet. It will ask you to have the difficult performance conversations before you feel ready, to build trust before you build change, and to define your leadership brand not as a performance but as a genuine expression of who you actually are.

None of that is easy. All of it is worth it.

A NOTE ON THE POST–M&A CONTEXT

A significant portion of my first-90-day experiences have come not from clean role transitions but from mergers and acquisitions — entering organizations that are mid-integration, mid-restructure, or mid-recovery from the last round of both. If that is your context, the complexity you are navigating is genuinely different from a standard leadership transition. You are stepping into a team that may have already been through multiple rounds of change. You are inheriting trust that has been damaged by processes you didn't design. You are operating in an environment where the informal power structure has been scrambled and the cultural norms are in active negotiation. The listening phase matters even more. The trust-building phase is harder and longer. The change management work is more politically charged and more emotionally loaded. The frameworks in this guide apply throughout — and where the M&A context creates specific wrinkles, I have called them out directly. Section 2.4 on navigating inherited change is especially relevant. Start there if you need to.

Who This Guide Is For

This guide is written for mid-level and senior leaders stepping into new roles — whether that means a new organization, a new mandate within an existing one, or a newly formed team in the wake of a merger or restructure.

It is not written for first-time managers, though many of the principles apply. It assumes you already know how to lead — that you have been doing it for years and that you are good at it. What it offers is a structured, honest, Whole Human approach to the specific challenge of the first 90 days: a window that is simultaneously the most information-rich and the most pressure-filled of any leadership transition.

You have 90 days to set the conditions for everything that follows. Not to have all the answers — you won't. Not to have built the perfect team or the perfect strategy — you can't. But to have listened carefully enough, built trust deliberately enough, and shown up authentically enough that your team is ready to follow you into Phase Two.

That is what this guide is for.

> **You have 90 days to set the conditions for everything that follows. Not to have all the answers. To have earned the right to lead.**

How This Guide Is Structured

The guide is organized into three phases that mirror the real arc of a leadership transition:

1. **Phase One: Days 1–30 — Listen & Learn.** Know the business before you fix it. Find the Unseen Employees. Understand your own default leadership style under pressure.

2. **Phase Two: Days 31–60 — Assess & Connect.** Form your honest diagnosis of the business and the people. Build the trust that makes change possible. Navigate what was already in motion when you arrived.

3. **Phase Three: Days 61–90 — Plan & Commit.** Build your strategy, present your plan, establish your leadership brand, and set your team up to perform long after Day 90.

Each section combines narrative — including stories from my own career — with practical frameworks, self-assessment tools, templates, and action planning pages. The workbook elements are designed to be completed as you go, not after the fact. The most valuable thing you can do with this guide is use it in real time, not read it in advance and put it on the shelf.

A note on the stories: all names of colleagues and team members in the examples have been changed. The situations are real. The lessons are harder-won than any of them probably suggest in print.

One more thing before we start.

I became the Turtle — the leader who leads with both toughness and humanity, who brings their whole self to work instead of hiding behind a professional shell. It took time, and it took work, and there were more Iron Maiden moments along the way than I'm proud of — moments where I armored up, shut down, and led from behind a wall instead of from the front. But I got there. And the leaders who have used these frameworks — in coaching, in workshops, in the organizations I have been part of — have got there too.

You will too. Now let's get to work.

LISTEN & LEARN

SECTION 1.1: KNOW THE BUSINESS BEFORE YOU FIX IT

You've been hired. The ink is dry, the announcement is out, and everyone is watching to see what you do next. The pressure to prove yourself is real. And it will absolutely lead you straight off a cliff if you let it.

The single biggest mistake new leaders make in the first 30 days isn't moving too slowly. It's moving before they understand what they're actually stepping into.

You cannot fix what you don't understand. And understanding takes longer than most leaders give it.

> **You cannot fix what you don't understand. And understanding takes longer than most leaders give it.**

The first 30 days are an information-gathering mission. Full stop. Your job is not to lead yet — it's to listen, observe, and learn. This section gives you the framework to do that systematically, so that when you do start making decisions, they're grounded in reality, not assumptions.

Start With the Business, Not the People

Most leaders default to people first — and that instinct isn't wrong. But if you walk into a business without understanding what it actually does, how it makes money, and where it's under pressure, you will misread every people conversation you have. Culture, engagement, and performance don't exist in a vacuum. They exist in the context of a business reality. Know that reality first.

Here's what you need to understand in the first 30 days:

- What does this organization actually sell? Not the elevator pitch — the real answer. What are the products or services, how are they differentiated, and what do customers actually buy them for?

- How does revenue flow? Where does it come from, who owns it, and where are the pressure points?

- What does the P&L look like? You don't need to be a CFO, but you need to understand the headline numbers: revenue, margin, cost structure, and where performance is tracking vs. plan.

- What's the org structure — formally and informally? The org chart tells you reporting lines. It does not tell you where the real decisions get made, who has influence, and who's been around long enough to know where the bodies are buried.

- What are the strategic priorities? What has leadership committed to delivering, and by when?

- What does "good" look like here? Every organization has its own definition of success. Find out what's being measured, and why.

The Org Chart vs. the Real Power Map

Here's something they don't put in the onboarding package: the organizational chart and the real power structure of a business are rarely the same thing.

The org chart shows you who reports to whom. The real power map tells you who people actually go to when they need a decision made, whose opinion carries weight in a room, who's been here through three leadership changes and knows where everything lives, and who has the relationships that make things happen.

In your first 30 days, you are mapping both. You need the official structure — and you need the unofficial one. The latter will tell you more about how to lead effectively in this organization than any briefing document ever will.

Pay attention to who gets referenced in conversations. Who do people credit with getting things done? Who do they mention when something went wrong? Who do they go quiet about? Those are your signals.

> **The org chart shows you who reports to whom. The real power map tells you who actually runs the place.**

Ask More Than You Answer

This is not the time to tell people what you've done elsewhere, share your vision, or signal the changes you're planning to make. All of that comes later — much later. Right now, your primary job is to ask great questions and actually listen to the answers.

Not performative listening. Real listening — where you are absorbing what someone is telling you, noticing what they're not saying, and paying attention to where the energy is in the room.

The best questions in this phase are open-ended, curious, and non-threatening:

- "What's working really well here that I should make sure I protect?"

- "Where are the biggest frustrations for your team right now?"

- "What's something you wish the last leader had understood sooner?"

- "If you could change one thing about how this organization operates, what would it be?"

- "What would success look like for you in the next 12 months?"

You will hear contradictions. You will hear different versions of the same story from different people. That's not a problem — it's data. It tells you about the gaps, the tensions, and the competing narratives that you'll eventually need to navigate. Write it all down.

What You're Actually Building in Phase One

By the end of Day 30, you should be able to answer the following without looking anything up:

- What this business sells and who buys it

- Where revenue comes from and where the cracks are

- How the org is structured — formally and in practice

- Who the key influencers are, at every level

- What the strategic priorities are and what's at risk

- What the culture actually feels like — not what it says on the wall

If you can't answer those questions clearly and confidently by Day 30, you have more listening to do before you start planning. That's not a failure. That's self-awareness — one of the most valuable things a new leader can bring to the table.

Template: Business Immersion Tracker

Complete this tracker during your first 30 days. Use it to organize what you learn across each domain — and to identify the gaps that still need filling.

Primary Products / Services	*What does this organization sell? What's the core value proposition?*
Revenue Model	*How does money flow in? What are the primary revenue streams?*
Key Clients / Customers	*Who are the top accounts? What do they value most?*
Competitive Landscape	*Who are the main competitors? What's the differentiation?*
P&L Headline Numbers	*Revenue, margin, cost structure — what's tracking vs. plan?*
Strategic Priorities	*What has leadership committed to delivering this year?*
Performance Gaps	*Where is the business underperforming? What's been tried?*
Current Initiatives	*What major projects or transformations are already in flight?*

Biggest Risks	*What's the leadership team most worried about?*
Definition of Success	*How is "good" defined here? What gets measured and celebrated?*

Template: Stakeholder Map — Who Holds Power, Who Holds Knowledge

Map every key stakeholder across two dimensions: their formal authority (org chart) and their real influence (who people actually listen to). Note what they care about, your current relationship status, and what you need from them in the first 90 days.

Name / Role	Formal Authority	Real Influence	Status
	High / Med / Low	*High / Med / Low*	*Ally / Neutral / Watch*
	High / Med / Low	*High / Med / Low*	*Ally / Neutral / Watch*
	High / Med / Low	*High / Med / Low*	*Ally / Neutral / Watch*
	High / Med / Low	*High / Med / Low*	*Ally / Neutral / Watch*

	High / Med / Low	High / Med / Low	Ally / Neutral / Watch
	High / Med / Low	High / Med / Low	Ally / Neutral / Watch
	High / Med / Low	High / Med / Low	Ally / Neutral / Watch
	High / Med / Low	High / Med / Low	Ally / Neutral / Watch

Add a notes column or separate page for each stakeholder as needed. What do they care about most? What's their history with this team? What do they need to see from you to trust you?

REFLECTION: END OF WEEK TWO

Take 20 minutes at the end of your second week to answer these questions honestly. Write your answers down — don't just think them.

- What do I now understand about this business that I didn't two weeks ago?

- What assumptions did I arrive with that have already been challenged?

- Where are the biggest gaps in my understanding right now?

- Who do I still need to spend time with before the end of Day 30?

- Am I spending more time listening or talking? What does that tell me?

Know What You're Walking Into

Not every new leadership role is the same — and the first mistake many leaders make is treating them like they are. Michael Watkins, author of The First 90 Days, offers a useful diagnostic called the STARS framework that categorizes the situation a leader inherits into one of five types: Start-up, Turnaround, Accelerated Growth, Realignment, or Sustaining Success.

It's worth knowing which one you're in — because each demands a different approach in those first 30 days. A turnaround calls for urgency and rapid diagnosis. A realignment requires patience and careful political navigation. Sustaining success means your biggest risk is fixing things that aren't broken.

Through the lens of Whole Human Leadership, this matters even more. The way you show up — how you balance critical thinking with emotional intelligence, how much you listen versus move — should be calibrated to the reality you've inherited. The Turtle doesn't swim the same way in every body of water.

Before Day One, ask yourself honestly: what kind of situation am I actually stepping into? Your answer shapes everything that follows.

Section 1.1 Key Takeaways

- The first 30 days are a listening and learning mission — not a proving ground.

- Understand the business before you form opinions about the people.

- The org chart and the real power map are two different things. You need both.

- Ask open-ended questions and write everything down. Contradictions are data, not noise.

- Know what type of situation you've inherited — it changes how you lead from Day One.

- By Day 30, you should be able to articulate the business clearly, honestly, and without notes.

Coming Up in Section 1.2: *The Unseen Organization — why your listening tour has to go beyond your direct reports, and how to find the people most leaders overlook.*

SECTION 1.2: THE UNSEEN ORGANIZATION

You've done your stakeholder mapping. You've met the senior team, walked the floor, and sat through the briefings. You think you have a reasonable picture of who's who.

You don't. Not yet.

Every organization has a layer that doesn't show up on any org chart, doesn't get introduced in your onboarding schedule, and rarely makes it onto anyone's radar until they've either left — or until something goes wrong. I call them the Unseen Employees. And finding them in your first 30 days is one of the highest-leverage moves a new leader can make.

This isn't a soft, feel-good exercise. It's a strategic imperative. The people most leaders overlook are often the ones who know exactly why the last three initiatives failed, why the top performer is quietly updating their resume, and where the real operational risk is hiding. They hold institutional knowledge that can't be bought, briefed, or Googled.

Miss them, and you'll spend the next six months discovering things you could have learned in Week Two.

The people most leaders overlook are often the ones who know exactly why the last three initiatives failed.

The Story Behind the Framework: David

Early in my career, before my first COO role, I was leading a contact centre operation with significant staffing and retention problems — the kind that every 24/7 environment seems to breed. My job was to figure out what was working on the high-performing teams and transplant it to the ones that were struggling.

The answer turned out to be sitting at a desk on the night shift. His name was David. A retired Canadian Football League linebacker — Grey Cup rings and all — who had taken a call centre job to support his family after his playing days ended. Gregarious, warm, and effortlessly good with people, he had quietly transformed the morale of everyone around him simply by showing up as himself.

Most of his supervisors had barely spoken to him. Some of his colleagues kept their distance, put off by his stature or, frankly, their own bias. But the people who actually spent time with David — including my then-partner Dee, who worked the same shift — knew exactly what he was worth.

I noticed. I invested time in understanding what he wanted to accomplish. And a couple of years later, when I had an opening for a client account manager, I hired him — not because his resume was the strongest in the pile, but because I already knew the thing no resume can tell you: how he made people feel, how he solved problems, and how he showed up under pressure.

David went on to build a second career that lasted twenty years. I played a small role in making that possible. But the bigger lesson for me was this: he was always there. I just had to look.

> **He was always there. I just had to look.**

Who Are the Unseen Employees?

The Unseen Employee isn't a type of person — it's a condition. It's what happens when an organization's culture, hiring habits, or leadership blind spots cause valuable people to go unnoticed, underutilized, or underestimated.

In your first 30 days, they might look like any of the following:

- The person who's been in the same role for eight years and knows every system, every workaround, and every client quirk — but has never been asked for their opinion in a strategic meeting.

- The high performer on a team whose manager takes credit for everything they produce.

- The quiet contributor who documents everything meticulously and is invisible precisely because they never cause problems.

- The person who was passed over for promotion three times and stopped advocating for themselves, but never stopped doing excellent work.

- The team member from a background different from the majority of the leadership group, whose perspective is rarely sought and whose ideas are rarely credited.

- The frontline employee who speaks to customers every day and has a clearer picture of your biggest product problems than anyone in the boardroom.

None of these people will introduce themselves to you as "the person leadership keeps overlooking." You have to go find them; deliberately, with open eyes and without the filter of whoever has been chosen to brief you.

Why Role Transitions Miss Them

It isn't malice. It's architecture. The way most onboarding is structured, new leaders spend the majority of their first 30 days with the people who already have proximity to power — direct reports, senior stakeholders, functional heads. These are important conversations. But they represent a single layer of a much more complex picture.

There are a few patterns I've seen consistently that cause new leaders to miss the Unseen Employee:

- Gravitating toward people who remind you of yourself — same background, same communication style, same energy. Comfortable, yes. Complete, no. **Pattern matching.**

- In any organization, some people are very good at being visible. Visible isn't the same as valuable. The person who dominates every meeting may not be the person who actually knows what's going on. **Defaulting to the loudest voices.**

- Whoever scheduled your onboarding decided who you'd meet. That list reflects their priorities and their blind spots — not necessarily yours. **Trusting the introduction list.**

- When you're under pressure to demonstrate early competence, slowing down to talk to someone three levels below you in the hierarchy can feel like a luxury. It isn't. It's due diligence. **Moving too fast.**

- This one's worth naming directly. Research consistently shows that leaders are more likely to notice, mentor, and sponsor people who look and sound like them. If your team is diverse and your attention isn't, that's a gap — and it's yours to close. **Unconscious bias.**

The Whole Human Leadership Lens

Whole Human Leadership asks you to see people fully — not just the version of them that shows up on a performance review or a seating chart. The Turtle doesn't swim with a bale by accident. It actively looks for the crew.

In your first 30 days, that means extending your listening tour beyond the obvious. It means sitting with the people who answer the phones, process the transactions, manage the accounts, and keep the operation running day to day. It means asking your direct reports who they think is underutilized. It means noticing who's in the room when a problem gets solved — and who never gets invited.

It also means checking yourself. What assumptions are you carrying about who is worth your time? What does your calendar in Week One actually say about whose perspective you've sought out? Those are hard questions. They're also the right ones.

The Unseen Employee isn't a problem to be solved after you've settled in. They're information you need right now, in Phase One, before you form your conclusions about what this organization is and what it needs.

> **The Turtle doesn't build a high-performing team by accident. It actively looks for the crew.**

How to Run a Real Listening Tour

A listening tour is not a meet-and-greet. It's a structured information-gathering exercise with a specific goal: to get a complete, unfiltered picture of the organization from multiple vantage points. Here's how to do it right:

- Schedule conversations with people two and three levels down. Not to skip the chain of command — but to understand what the view looks like from the front line. **Go beyond your direct reports.**

- Consistency lets you compare answers and spot patterns. Where people agree, you have signal. Where they contradict each other, you have tension worth understanding. **Ask the same core questions of everyone.**

- People will tell you what they think you want to hear unless you explicitly signal that you want the unvarnished truth. Say it out loud: "I'm here to listen and learn, not to judge or report back." **Create psychological safety from the first sentence.**

- Pay attention to what people light up about and what makes them go quiet. Both are telling you something. **Follow the energy.**

- Jot down themes and patterns after the conversation, not during it. Eye contact and presence matter more than a perfect transcript. **Take notes — but not in a way that makes people feel they're being documented.**

- The best signal you can send to an Unseen Employee is a second conversation. It says: I heard you, I remembered, and I came back. **Go back.**

Action Planning Page: Your Day 1–30 Listening Tour

Use this planner to map out who you will meet beyond the standard onboarding list. Aim for at least 8–10 conversations outside your direct reports and senior stakeholders in the first 30 days.

Frontline / operational roles	*Who are 2–3 people in day-to-day delivery who have been here 3+ years?*
Cross-functional peers	*Who leads functions adjacent to yours that you'll need to work with?*
Longest-tenured team members	*Who has the most institutional memory? Who has seen leaders come and go?*
Recent hires (under 12 months)	*What did they notice in their first weeks that veterans no longer see?*
People passed over internally	*Who applied for this role or a similar one and didn't get it? What do they know?*
Client-facing staff	*Who speaks to customers every day? What are they hearing that leadership isn't?*

Support / enabling functions	Ops, finance, HR, IT — who holds the operational reality together?
Anyone your direct reports avoid mentioning	*Notice the omissions. They're data too.*

Template: Core Listening Tour Questions
Ask these questions consistently across every conversation. The patterns in the answers are what you're looking for — not any single response.
On the business: *What's working really well right now that I should make sure I protect?*
On the business: *Where are the biggest frustrations or friction points in how we operate?*
On the team: *Who do people go to when they need something done — and why?*
On the team: *Who do you think is underutilized or underestimated here?*
On leadership: *What's something you wish the last leader had understood sooner?*
On leadership: *What would make your job meaningfully easier in the next 6 months?*
On culture: *How would you describe the culture here to someone who was thinking about joining?*
On culture: *Is there anything people say behind closed doors that never gets said in meetings?*
Open: *What haven't I asked you that I probably should have?*

SELF-ASSESSMENT: CHECKING YOUR BLIND SPOTS

Answer these questions honestly before you finalize your Day 30 listening tour. Uncomfortable answers are the useful ones.

- Look at your calendar for the first two weeks. What percentage of your conversations were with people at your level or above?

- Who introduced you to the people you've met so far? Whose agenda does that list reflect?

- Is there a demographic pattern in the people you've sought out? Would a diverse team recognize themselves in your first 30 days?

- Who have you walked past — literally or figuratively — without stopping to engage?

- Name one person in this organization who you suspect has been overlooked. What's your plan to change that?

- Are you making time for people who challenge your assumptions, or only for people who confirm them?

There are no right answers here — only honest ones. The point isn't to feel good about your first 30 days. It's to see them clearly enough to do the next 30 better.

Section 1.2 Key Takeaways

- Every organization has an Unseen layer. Your job in Phase One is to find it before you form your conclusions.

- The people who don't make the onboarding list often hold the most valuable institutional knowledge.

- A listening tour isn't a calendar exercise — it's a strategic discipline. Structure it, and go beyond the obvious.

- Consistent questions across conversations reveal patterns. Patterns are where the real intelligence lives.

- Check your own blind spots deliberately. Whose perspective have you sought? Whose have you skipped?

- The Turtle builds its bale intentionally — by seeing people fully, not just conveniently.

Coming Up in Section 1.3: *Know Yourself Before You Lead Others — how your default leadership style shows up under pressure in a new environment, and why self-awareness is a business-critical skill in the first 30 days.*

LISTEN & LEARN

SECTION 1.3: KNOW YOURSELF BEFORE YOU LEAD OTHERS

Every new role is a mirror. And most leaders don't look into it nearly carefully enough.

You arrive with a track record, a set of instincts, and a default way of operating that has been shaped by every role, every boss, every crisis, and every failure you've navigated to get here. Some of those instincts will serve you brilliantly in this new context. Some will get you into trouble. The problem is, you won't know which is which until you've examined them — and a new role has a way of stress-testing everything you think you know about yourself, often before you're ready.

Self-awareness isn't a soft skill. In the first 30 days of a new leadership role, it's a business-critical one. How you show up sets the tone for everything that follows. The habits you establish in Phase One — how you communicate, how you make decisions, how you handle uncertainty, how you treat people — become the template your team uses to understand who you are and what you expect. You don't get a second first impression. And you don't get to unring the bell of a bad first 30 days.

This section is about getting honest with yourself before any of that happens.

> **Self-awareness isn't a soft skill. In the first 30 days of a new role, it's a business-critical one.**

The Story Behind the Framework: The Iron Maiden

Early in my career, I was what my colleagues nicknamed the Iron Maiden. I didn't know it at the time — or rather, I knew the nickname, but I hadn't fully grasped what it meant about how I was showing up.

I was buttoned up, results-focused, and relentlessly professional. I left my personal life at the door because I believed compartmentalizing was a strength. I made hard decisions without flinching and kept my emotions tightly under wraps. In my mind, I was exactly what a senior leader was supposed to be.

What I didn't realize was that the version of me my colleagues encountered at work was a shell — a carefully constructed, armour-plated version that kept the whole human safely out of sight. It took a throwaway comment from a colleague — who told me she'd assumed I was the type of person who laughed at people who cried at movies — to make me understand how completely I'd hidden myself. And what that was costing me as a leader.

The Iron Maiden wasn't who I was. She was who I thought I needed to be. And the gap between those two things was doing real damage — to my team, to my relationships, and ultimately to my own effectiveness.

Here's what I know now that I didn't know then: the qualities I was suppressing — empathy, vulnerability, emotional connection — weren't weaknesses. They were the very things that would eventually make me a far more powerful leader. The Turtle I became wasn't softer than the Iron Maiden. She was stronger. Because the strength that comes from knowing yourself is a completely different thing from the strength that comes from armour.

As a new leader stepping into a role, you will feel pressure to project certainty, competence, and control. Some of that is legitimate — your team needs to feel confident in you. But there is a version of that pressure that will push you toward the Iron Maiden: performative toughness, emotional distance, the reflexive need to have all the answers. Watch for it. It's one of the most common failure modes of the first 90 days.

The qualities I was suppressing weren't weaknesses. They were the things that would make me a far more powerful leader.

Your Default Leadership Style Under Pressure

You have a default. Every leader does. It's the mode you revert to when things get uncertain, when you're under pressure, or when you don't yet have enough information to lead with confidence. And a new role is almost entirely made up of those conditions.

Your default isn't necessarily your best self. It's your most automatic self — the version of you that runs on instinct before your more considered, intentional leadership kicks in. Understanding what that looks like is the work of this section.

Common default patterns in new leaders under pressure include:

- Fills the uncertainty gap by doing — producing, delivering, proving. Moves fast, takes on too much, and struggles to delegate. The team sees energy and output, but also chaos and a leader who doesn't trust them yet. **The Overachiever.**

- Fills the uncertainty gap by seeking approval — checking in constantly, adjusting their position based on whoever they spoke to last, hesitant to commit. The team sees indecision and wonders who's actually in charge. **The Validator.**

- Arrives with the answers already formed. Diagnoses problems before they've listened, brings solutions from their last role, and moves to change things before they've earned the trust to do so. The team feels dismissed. **The Fixer.**

- The Iron Maiden. Keeps people at a professional distance, defaults to formality and process, confuses emotional control with emotional unavailability. The team respects the capability but doesn't feel seen. **The Armour-Wearer.**

- Avoids difficult conversations in the early weeks to preserve goodwill. Defers too much, hedges too much, over-reassures. Builds short-term comfort at the expense of long-term credibility. **The People-Pleaser.**

None of these defaults are fatal. All of them are manageable — once you can see them. The goal isn't to eliminate your instincts. It's to know which ones to trust and which ones to actively override.

The CT + EI Balance in a New Environment

In Whole Human Leadership, the two foundational competencies are Critical Thinking (CT) and Emotional Intelligence (EI). Both matter in Phase One — but they show up differently, and the balance between them is something most new leaders get wrong.

Critical Thinking is your shell — the analytical, objective, fact-based part of your leadership that protects you from making decisions on incomplete information or emotional reaction. In a new role, you need it to assess what you're seeing clearly, without letting your prior experiences or assumptions colour the picture.

Emotional Intelligence is your body — the part of your leadership that reads the room, builds trust, regulates your own emotional responses, and creates the conditions for honest conversation. In a new role, you need it to connect with people before you can influence them, and to understand the human dynamics underneath the operational surface.

The trap most new leaders fall into is over-indexing on one at the expense of the other. Leaders who lead exclusively with CT in Phase One come across as analytical but cold — technically competent but hard to follow. Leaders who lead exclusively with EI come across as warm but directionless — likeable but not yet credible.

The Turtle holds both. You can read a P&L and read a room. You can make a hard call and make people feel heard in the process. That's not a contradiction — it's Whole Human Leadership. And it starts with knowing which one you tend to reach for first.

> **You can read a P&L and read a room. That's not a contradiction — it's Whole Human Leadership.**

The Iron Maiden vs. The Turtle: Know Where You're Starting

One of the most useful things you can do before the end of Day 30 is get honest about where you are on the spectrum between the Iron Maiden and the Turtle. Not where you want to be. Where you actually are — right now, in this new environment, under the specific pressures of this role.

The table below maps the key behavioural differences. Read it without judgment. Your starting point is just data — it tells you what to work on, not who you are.

The Iron Maiden vs. The Turtle: A Behavioural Comparison

Read each row and mark honestly which column better describes how you currently show up — especially under pressure or in unfamiliar situations.

The Iron Maiden (Incomplete Leader)	The Turtle (Whole Human Leader)
Keeps personal context out of all professional interactions	Shares relevant personal context to build understanding and connection
Leads with authority and hierarchy	Leads with collaboration and shared ownership
Measures success primarily through business metrics	Measures success through both people and business outcomes
Avoids or delays difficult conversations	Addresses performance and conflict promptly and directly

Reacts to emotion — either suppressing it or expressing it impulsively	Regulates emotion through CT + EI, responds rather than reacts
Arrives in a new role with solutions already formed	Arrives with questions and a structured learning agenda
Seeks credit for team outcomes	Attributes success to the team, takes accountability for failures
Builds relationships transactionally	Invests in relationships as a long-term leadership asset
Treats vulnerability as weakness	Uses vulnerability strategically to build trust and psychological safety
Hires and promotes in their own likeness	Actively seeks diversity of background, thought, and experience

Self-Assessment: Your WHL Baseline — Day 1

Rate yourself honestly against each Whole Human Leadership trait as you are right now — not as you aspire to be. This is your starting point. You will revisit this at Day 30 and again at Day 90.

WHL Trait / Behaviour	Rarely	Sometimes	Consistently
I listen more than I talk in new situations	☐	☐	☐
I regulate my emotions before responding under pressure	☐	☐	☐
I ask open-ended questions before forming conclusions	☐	☐	☐

I acknowledge what I don't know without losing credibility	☐	☐	☐
I invest time in people regardless of their level or title	☐	☐	☐
I create space for others to disagree with me	☐	☐	☐
I take accountability for team outcomes — including failures	☐	☐	☐
I lead with my values, even when it's uncomfortable	☐	☐	☐
I adapt my communication style to the person I'm talking to	☐	☐	☐
I recognize and actively work against my own biases	☐	☐	☐
I bring my whole self to work — not just my professional shell	☐	☐	☐
I build trust before I build change	☐	☐	☐

Where you marked 'Rarely' or 'Sometimes' — those are your development priorities for Phase One. They're not flaws. They're the gaps between where you are and where the Turtle operates. Circle them. Come back to them in Section 3.3 when you build your leadership brand.

REFLECTION: THE NICKNAME YOU DON'T WANT

My colleagues called me the Iron Maiden. It wasn't who I was — it was who I'd allowed the environment to make me. Before you finish Phase One, sit with these questions:

- What nickname might your new team give you based on how you've shown up so far? Is that who you want to be?

- What parts of yourself are you leaving at the door — and is that a strategic choice or an unconscious habit?

- When did you last feel like the Turtle in a professional setting? What made that possible?

- What's the version of you that this new role is most likely to bring out under pressure? Is that the version you want your team to experience?

- Write your Whole Human Leader statement: "In this role, I intend to be known for…"

You'll formalize this into your Personal Leadership Statement in Section 3.3. For now, just write the first honest version of it.

Section 1.3 Key Takeaways

- Every new role stress-tests your default leadership style — usually before you're ready for it.

- The Iron Maiden isn't a villain. She's a leader who hasn't yet given themselves permission to show up whole. Recognize her if she appears.

- Self-awareness is a business-critical skill in Phase One — not a personal development exercise.

- CT and EI work together. Over-indexing on either one in a new environment will cost you credibility.

- Your WHL Baseline is just data — it tells you what to develop, not who you are.

- The habits and tone you set in the first 30 days become the template your team uses to understand you. Make them intentional.

COMPLETING PHASE ONE

By the end of Day 30, you should be able to say:

- I understand what this business sells, how it makes money, and where it's under pressure.

- I know the formal org structure and the real power map — and they are not the same thing.

- I have gone beyond my direct reports and identified people the organization is underutilizing.

- I know my default leadership style under pressure — and I've identified what to watch.

- I have a WHL Baseline that tells me where to focus my development in Phases Two and Three.

If you can answer yes to all five — you're ready for Phase Two.

Coming Up in Phase Two: *Days 31–60 — Assess & Connect. Now that you understand the business and the people, it's time to form your honest assessment, build the trust that makes change possible, and start laying the groundwork for your strategy.*

ASSESS & CONNECT

SECTION 2.1: DIAGNOSING THE BUSINESS: WHAT'S ACTUALLY WORKING

You've spent 30 days listening. You've mapped the business, found the Unseen Employees, and taken an honest look at how you show up under pressure. That was Phase One — information gathering, with judgment firmly suspended.

Phase Two is different. The listening doesn't stop, but now you start forming views. Carefully, honestly, and with full awareness that your diagnosis will shape every decision you make in the next 60 days. Get it right, and you build your strategy on solid ground. Get it wrong — or worse, let your preconceptions substitute for actual analysis — and you'll spend months fixing problems you created.

The most common diagnostic mistake new leaders make isn't moving too slowly. It's confusing what they were told with what's actually true. In Phase One, everyone had an agenda — consciously or not. The senior leader who briefed you on the team had opinions baked into every sentence. The direct report who was most eager to get time with you had something to gain. Even the quiet observations you made were filtered through the lens of what you were looking for.

Phase Two is where you test all of that. You stop receiving the narrative and start interrogating it.

The Story Behind the Framework: Death by a Thousand Cuts

Early in my career I sat across from the North American President of a company I was working for and told him directly: "Tim, this death by a thousand cuts has to stop."

We had completed six acquisitions in eighteen months, and the management strategy was to lay people off in incremental drips — small rounds, over and over, each one landing on a team that had barely recovered from the last. The result was a culture of panic. People spending company time updating their resumes. Managers too distracted by their own job security to lead their teams. A business that was nominally executing but was psychologically disintegrating underneath the surface.

The data said we were hitting our cost targets. The culture said we were in crisis. Both things were true — and only one of them was showing up in the reports Tim was reading.

That gap — between what the numbers say and what the organization is actually experiencing — is one of the most dangerous blind spots a leader can have. And it almost always becomes visible in Phase Two, if you know how to look for it.

A complete business diagnosis reads three layers simultaneously: what the data says, what people say, and what actually happens. They are rarely the same thing. Where they diverge is exactly where your most important work lives.

> **A complete diagnosis reads three layers: what the data says, what people say, and what actually happens. Where they diverge is where your work lives.**

The Three Layers of an Honest Diagnosis

Most leaders are comfortable with Layer One. Layer Three is where the real intelligence is.

- Revenue, margin, headcount, attrition, productivity metrics, customer satisfaction scores, pipeline. The numbers tell you what is measurable. They do not tell you why, or whether what is being measured actually matters. Read them first — then hold them lightly. **What the data says.**

- What you heard in Phase One. The narratives, the concerns, the things people said when they thought they were being candid. This layer is valuable and unreliable in equal measure. It reflects perception, politics, and personal agenda as much as it reflects reality. Cross-reference everything. **What people say.**

- The hardest layer to read and the most important. How do decisions actually get made here? Who really has influence? What gets rewarded, tolerated, or quietly ignored? What does a bad day in this organization look like, and how does leadership respond? This layer is visible only through direct observation over time — which is exactly why 30 days of active listening was not optional. **What actually happens**.

The discipline of Phase Two is holding all three layers simultaneously and noting where they align and where they contradict. Alignment gives you confidence. Contradiction gives you your most important diagnostic questions.

Reading Culture as Data

Culture is the most under-diagnosed business variable in most organizations. It's treated as soft — a footnote to strategy, a talking point for the all-hands. In reality, culture is an operating infrastructure. It determines how fast decisions get made, whether people speak up when something is wrong, whether your best performers stay, and whether your strategy gets executed or quietly subverted.

As a new leader, you have a narrow window of time in which you can see the culture clearly — before you become part of it and stop noticing it. Use it.

Here are the cultural signals worth reading deliberately in Phase Two:

- Are they made in the room, or ratified after the fact? Who needs to be consulted before anything moves? Is speed valued or is consensus the price of action? **How are decisions made?**

- Is disagreement surfaced and resolved, or does it go underground and fester? Do people say what they think in meetings, or save it for the corridor afterward? **How is conflict handled?**

- Look at what leadership publicly recognizes. Revenue? Individual heroics? Process compliance? Team outcomes? What gets celebrated tells you what this culture actually values — not what it claims to value. **What gets celebrated?**

- Every culture has things it allows that it shouldn't. The toxic top performer who everyone works around. The manager whose team has 40% attrition every year. The senior leader who takes credit and assigns blame. What is tolerated here — and by whom? **What gets tolerated?**

- Does news — especially bad news — travel up the hierarchy quickly and accurately? Or does it get filtered, softened, and delayed? The quality of information flow is one of the most reliable indicators of organizational health. **How does information flow?**

- Not to you — around you. The energy in a room when a senior leader's name comes up. The things people say in the last five minutes of a conversation when they've relaxed. Pay attention. **How do people talk about leadership?**

The WHL Lens: Using CT and EI Together

Diagnosing a business requires both sides of the Turtle. Critical thinking keeps your analysis objective — it stops you from confusing a compelling narrative with evidence, or a likeable person with a high performer. Emotional intelligence keeps your diagnosis complete — it ensures you're reading the human operating system underneath the org chart, not just the formal one.

Neither is sufficient alone. A pure CT diagnosis will give you an accurate picture of the measurable reality and miss the cultural dynamics that will determine whether any of your plans actually land. A pure EI diagnosis will give you a rich sense of the human environment and potentially miss the structural or financial realities that are driving it.

The discipline is to use them in sequence. Start with the data — let the numbers tell their story without the emotional filter. Then layer in the human intelligence — what you observed, what you heard, what you sensed in rooms. Then ask yourself where the two pictures agree, where they conflict, and what would explain the gaps.

That intersection is your diagnosis.

> **Start with the data. Layer in the human intelligence. The intersection is your diagnosis.**

Quick Wins vs. Structural Change: Know the Difference

One of the most important outputs of your Phase Two diagnosis is a clear distinction between what can be fixed quickly and what requires structural change over time. Getting this wrong in either direction costs you.

Moving too fast on structural change — before you've earned the trust and built the relationships to bring people with you — creates resistance that can derail even the right solution. Moving too slowly on visible quick wins — the kind that show your team you're paying attention and you're capable — leaves a credibility vacuum that other people will fill.

Quick wins are not about proving yourself. They're about demonstrating that you listen, you act, and you follow through. They're the evidence your team needs to decide whether to invest in you. The best quick wins in Phase Two are usually not dramatic. They're often small things that have been frustrating people for months that nobody with authority has bothered to fix.

Ask directly: "What's one thing that would make your team's work meaningfully easier that hasn't been addressed?" Then fix it. Quickly. Visibly. Without making a production of it.

Template: Business Health Diagnostic

Rate each domain Red (urgent attention needed), Yellow (monitoring required), or Green (healthy). Note your priority action for any Red or Yellow domain. Complete this by the end of Week Five.

Domain	Current State	Health	Your Priority Action
Revenue & Growth	*Is the business growing? Are the right revenue streams healthy?*	Red / Yellow / Green	
Margin & Cost Structure	*Is the P&L sustainable? Where is cost pressure building?*	Red / Yellow / Green	
Client / Customer Health	*Are key relationships stable? What's the retention and satisfaction picture?*	Red / Yellow / Green	

Pipeline & Market Position	*Is there a healthy pipeline? How does the competitive position look?*	🔴 🟡 🟢	
Operational Delivery	*Is the business executing on its commitments? Where are the failure points?*	🔴 🟡 🟢	
Team Performance	*Are the right people in the right roles? Where are the capability gaps?*	🔴 🟡 🟢	
Culture & Engagement	*Is the culture healthy? What does attrition and engagement data say?*	🔴 🟡 🟢	
Leadership Effectiveness	*Is the leadership team aligned and functional? Where are the tensions?*	🔴 🟡 🟢	
Process & Infrastructure	*Do the systems and processes support the work? What's breaking regularly?*	🔴 🟡 🟢	
Strategic Clarity	*Does the organization understand and believe in where it's going?*	🔴 🟡 🟢	

Template: What's Working / What's Broken / Quick Wins / Where the Bodies Are Buried

Complete this template by the end of Day 45. Be specific. Vague observations are not a diagnosis.

<table>
<tr><td>WHAT'S WORKING

Protect this. Build on it.</td><td>WHAT'S BROKEN

Fix this. But earn the right first.</td></tr>
<tr><td></td><td></td></tr>
<tr><td>QUICK WINS

Visible wins that build your credibility fast.</td><td>WHERE THE BODIES ARE BURIED

Know this. Move carefully. Don't step on it.</td></tr>
<tr><td></td><td></td></tr>
</table>

REFLECTION: TESTING YOUR DIAGNOSIS

Before you finalize your assessment and move to building trust and relationships in Section 2.2, pressure-test your diagnosis with these questions:

- What is the single biggest gap between what the organization thinks is true about itself and what you believe is actually true?

- Where have you been told something is working that your own observation suggests isn't? What's driving that gap?

- What is being tolerated here that shouldn't be? Who is allowing it — and why?

- What is one quick win you could deliver in the next two weeks that your team would immediately notice and value?

- What is one structural issue that needs to change — and that you are not yet in a position to change? What needs to happen first?

- Where might your own bias or prior experience be shaping your diagnosis? What would change if you were wrong?

Section 2.1 Key Takeaways

- Phase Two is where listening becomes assessment — and where your judgment finally goes to work.

- A complete diagnosis reads three layers: data, narrative, and observed reality. Where they diverge is where the real work lives.

- Culture is operating infrastructure, not a soft metric. Read it deliberately before you become part of it.

- Use CT to stay objective. Use EI to stay complete. The intersection of both is your diagnosis.

- Distinguish clearly between quick wins and structural change — and sequence them intentionally.

- Pressure-test your own diagnosis. Your prior experience and your desire to be right are both liabilities here.

Coming Up in Section 2.2: *Building Trust Before You Build Anything Else — why the leaders who move fastest in Phase Two are the ones who invested most deliberately in trust, and how to do that without losing your edge.*

ASSESS & CONNECT

SECTION 2.2: BUILDING TRUST BEFORE YOU BUILD ANYTHING ELSE

Every leader arrives in a new role with an agenda. You have things you want to change, initiatives you want to launch, a vision of what good looks like that you're quietly measuring this organization against. That's not a problem. That's leadership.

The problem is when the agenda arrives before the trust. And in most organizations, it does.

Trust is not a soft outcome. It is the operating condition that determines whether your ideas get executed or quietly ignored, whether your team tells you what's actually happening or tells you what they think you want to hear, and whether the people with real influence in this organization work with you or work around you. Without it, you are a leader in title only.

The research on leadership transitions is unambiguous on this point: the leaders who create the most sustainable change in their first 90 days are not the ones who moved fastest. They are the ones who invested most deliberately in building the relationships that made fast movement possible. Trust is not what you build after you've earned credibility. Trust is how you earn it.

> **Trust is not what you build after you've earned credibility. Trust is how you earn it.**

The Story Behind the Framework: Kate

When I was relocated to New York at 30 to lead North American operations for a company I'd joined less than two years earlier, I walked into a team of formidable New Yorkers who had every reason to be skeptical of me. I was young, I was Canadian, and I had limited experience in the travel industry — which was exactly the industry I was now supposed to be leading at scale.

Kate was a very important person on that team. She was a seasoned, fiercely respected 60-year-old New Yorker who managed one of our most significant client relationships. From the moment I met her, her eyes told me everything I needed to know: "Who is this woman half my age, and why should I listen to anything she says?"

I could have asserted authority. I had the title to do it. I could have come in with my agenda, my changes, my vision — and made it clear, professionally and efficiently, that this was the new direction and Kate was welcome to get on board or not. That is what the Iron Maiden would have done.

Instead, I took nearly a year to earn her trust. Not because I was slow, or unsure, or lacking in conviction — but because I understood that Kate's trust was not just personally valuable. It was organizationally essential. She was the person the rest of the legacy team watched. Where Kate went, they followed.

I invested time in understanding her expertise and publicly acknowledging it. I told her directly what I didn't know and where her knowledge complemented mine. I demonstrated that I was there to build with her, not around her. And I waited.

The moment I knew it had worked: a senior leadership meeting, another acquisition on the table, more restructuring ahead, voices in the room pushing back. Kate spoke up in my favour. A woman who had spent a year watching me carefully — testing me without ever saying she was testing me — decided I was worth defending. After that, the legacy team followed.

You cannot rush that. And you cannot manufacture it. You can only earn it — through consistency, through competence, through the quality of your attention, and through the courage to take accountability publicly when something goes wrong.

> **The moment Kate spoke up for me, I knew a year of patience had paid off. You cannot rush trust. You can only earn it.**

What Trust Actually Requires

Trust in a leadership context is not about being liked. It is about being predictable, credible, and safe to be honest with. Those three things together create the conditions in which people will follow you into uncertainty — which is, ultimately, what leadership asks of them.

- People need to know how you will behave — especially under pressure. If your mood, your priorities, and your standards shift based on the day or the audience, people will spend their energy managing you rather than doing their best work. Consistency is not rigidity. It is the foundation of safety. **Predictability.**

- You earn credibility not by claiming expertise but by demonstrating sound judgment, following through on commitments, and being honest about what you don't know. In a new role, credibility is built in small moments — the meeting where you said something accurate, the commitment you kept, the problem you solved without drama. **Credibility.**

- People need to believe that telling you the truth — about a problem, a mistake, a disagreement — will not cost them. This is the hardest element of trust to build and the easiest to destroy. It requires you to respond to bad news with curiosity rather than blame, to model the vulnerability that you're asking your team to show, and to take accountability publicly and visibly when things go wrong. **Psychological safety.**

These three elements build on each other and they build over time. There are no shortcuts. But there are deliberate practices that accelerate the process — and deliberate mistakes that derail it.

The Political Landscape: Influence, Resistance, and the Unofficial Power Structure

Trust-building in a new leadership role is not a neutral exercise. It happens inside a political landscape that was established long before you arrived, with factions, histories, loyalties, and agendas that you are only beginning to understand.

Every organization has an unofficial power structure that runs parallel to the formal one. In Phase One you mapped it — who has real influence, whose endorsement matters, who the blockers are. In Phase Two, you use that map to be strategic about where you invest your trust-building energy first.

Not all relationships carry equal weight. The senior leader who is formally your peer but informally the person everyone defers to is a higher priority than someone with a more visible title and less actual influence. The long-tenured team member who has survived four leadership transitions and has the institutional memory of the entire department is worth more of your time than the enthusiastic new hire who arrived the same week you did.

Be strategic without being cynical. Prioritizing relationships based on their organizational significance is not manipulation — it is competent leadership. The goal is to build a coalition of people who understand what you're trying to do and are willing to help you do it. That coalition is what makes change possible.

The resistors deserve attention too — not avoidance. The person who is most skeptical of you in Phase Two is often the most important person to understand. Their resistance is usually not personal. It is historical, structural, or self-protective. Understanding what's driving it — and addressing it directly, with patience and without capitulation — is one of the highest-leverage trust-building moves available to you.

> **The person most skeptical of you in Phase Two is often the most important person to understand.**

What Destroys Trust Faster Than Anything Else

Building trust takes months. Destroying it takes minutes. New leaders are particularly vulnerable to trust-destroying behaviours in Phase Two because they are still operating without full information, under significant pressure, and often with the instinct to prove themselves working against them.

Watch for these:

- In a new environment, people compare notes. They always do. Inconsistency of message is one of the fastest ways to lose credibility with an entire team simultaneously. **Saying one thing to one person and a different thing to another.**

- You have not yet done enough to own results. Be generous in attribution. Your team is watching how you handle success before they decide how much to invest in yours. **Taking credit for early wins that belong to the team.**

- New leaders are sometimes tempted to distance themselves from failures that pre-date them. Don't. Taking ownership — even for things you didn't cause — signals that you are a leader who stands with their team, not one who uses them as cover. **Avoiding accountability when something goes wrong.**

- Change without trust creates resistance. Even the right decision, made before people trust you enough to follow, can derail your first 90 days. **Moving too fast on visible changes before you've built the relationships to support them.**

- Cancelling one-on-ones, being distracted in meetings, failing to follow up on things you said you'd do. In a new role, your presence is a signal. Absence or distraction is read as disinterest — and disinterest is the beginning of disengagement. **Being inconsistently present.**

The 1:1 as a Trust-Building Instrument

Nothing builds trust faster than a well-run one-on-one — and nothing wastes an opportunity faster than a poorly run one. In Phase Two, your 1:1s are not status updates. They are the primary vehicle through which you demonstrate that you see people, that you listen, and that you follow through.

A trust-building 1:1 in Days 31–60 has a specific structure:

- Start with what's on their mind, not your agenda. Ask an open question and genuinely listen to the answer. This alone distinguishes you from most leaders they've had. **Open with them, not with you.**

- Not just outputs — what's energizing them, what's frustrating them, where they feel stuck. This is how you find the Unseen Employee signal inside a formal reporting relationship. **Ask about their work and their experience of it.**

- Not a performance of vulnerability — something real. A challenge you're navigating, something you've learned, a decision you're uncertain about. This is how you demonstrate that the Whole Human Leader isn't a character you play in all-hands meetings. **Share something of yourself.**

- Even small. Even simple. And then do it. The follow-through on a small commitment in a 1:1 is one of the highest-ROI trust-building moves available to a new leader. **Commit to something specific.**

- Not what the organization needs. What they need. This shifts the conversation from transactional to relational and signals that your leadership is in service of them, not just the other way around. **Close by asking what they need from you.**

Action Planning Page: Your Trust-Building Plan

Identify your 8–10 most important trust relationships in Phase Two. For each, assess the current trust level honestly, identify what they need to see from you specifically, and commit to a concrete action. Complete by end of Day 35.

Stakeholder	Current Trust Level	What They Need to See From You	Your Specific Action
	Low / Med / High		
	Low / Med / High		
	Low / Med / High		
	Low / Med / High		
	Low / Med / High		
	Low / Med / High		
	Low / Med / High		

Template: Political Landscape — Influence vs. Trust Matrix

Place your key stakeholders into the appropriate quadrant based on their real organizational influence (not their formal title) and your current trust relationship with them. This tells you where to invest your energy in Phase Two.

HIGH INFLUENCE | LOW TRUST	HIGH INFLUENCE | HIGH TRUST
Your most important trust-building priority. Invest here first.	*Protect and leverage these relationships. They are your coalition.*
Names / notes:	Names / notes:
LOW INFLUENCE | LOW TRUST	**LOW INFLUENCE | HIGH TRUST**
Monitor. Don't ignore — influence can shift.	*Allies in the making. Invest in them — they can grow.*
Names / notes:	Names / notes:

TEMPLATE: 1:1 MEETING FRAMEWORK — DAYS 31–60

Use this structure for every direct report 1:1 in Phase Two. Aim for weekly cadence. During your first 90–120 days, invest 45–60 minutes per session — the relationship capital you build in this window is worth the calendar cost. Once you're past that mark and trust is established, 30 minutes is a realistic and sufficient ongoing cadence. Your notes from each meeting feed directly into your team assessment in Section 2.3.

Open (10 min)

- What's on your mind right now — work or otherwise?
- What's been the best part of your week? What's been the hardest?

Their Work (20 min)

- What are you working on that you're most proud of right now?
- Where are you feeling blocked or under-resourced?
- What would make your work meaningfully easier that isn't currently in place?

Connection (10 min)

- What do you want to accomplish in this role in the next 12 months?
- What kind of leader do you do your best work for? What does that tell me about what you need from me?

Close (5 min) — Total: 45 min

- What do you need from me before we meet again?

- Commit to one specific action. Write it down. Do it.

After every 1:1, note: What did I learn? What did I commit to? What do I need to follow up on? Keep this record — it feeds your team assessment in Section 2.3. After Day 120, compress to a 30-minute cadence: 5 min open, 15 min their work, 5 min connection, 5 min close. Same structure, tighter time.

Section 2.2 Key Takeaways

- Trust is the operating condition that determines whether your leadership actually lands. Build it before you build anything else.

- Predictability, credibility, and psychological safety are the three pillars of trust. All three must be present.

- Map your political landscape and invest your trust-building energy strategically — prioritize influence over title.

- Resistors are information. Understand what's driving their resistance before you try to overcome it.

- The 1:1 is your most powerful trust-building instrument. Use it properly — not as a status update but as a genuine connection.

- Small commitments kept consistently are more trust-building than grand gestures. Follow through, every time.

Coming Up in Section 2.3: *Your People — Honest Assessment. Now that you've built the foundation of trust, it's time to assess your team with clear eyes — performance, potential, and fit — and have the conversations that set everyone up to succeed.*

SECTION 2.3: YOUR PEOPLE: HONEST ASSESSMENT

The most consequential decisions you will make as a new leader are not about strategy or structure. They are about people. Who is in the right role, who isn't, who has more to give than anyone is asking of them, and who has been quietly underperforming for longer than anyone wants to admit.

Getting this assessment right — and doing it with both honesty and humanity — is the work of Phase Two. Done well, it sets the foundation for everything in Phase Three: the strategy, the plan, and the leadership brand you build from it. Done poorly — or worse, avoided entirely — it leaves you leading a team whose real composition you don't fully understand, making decisions on incomplete information, and inheriting problems that compound over time.

This section is about forming a clear, honest, and fair picture of every person on your team. Not to judge them. Not to build a case for action you've already decided to take. But to understand what you actually have, so you can lead it effectively.

> **Getting the people assessment right — with honesty and humanity — is the work that makes everything else in Phase Three possible.**

The Stories Behind the Framework

I want to be upfront: when it comes to toxic top performers, I have more composite examples to draw from than I'd like to admit. Apparently, it's a recurring theme in corporate life. Who knew.

Let's start with the one that's easier to talk about — the underperformer — because it's the one most new leaders handle worst.

The Underperformer: The Mike Story

Early in my career, I hired someone — I'll call him Mike — into a role that required significant performance management capability. The team he was inheriting was struggling, and I was clear with him from the very first interview: this role would require difficult conversations, structured performance plans, and the ability to hold people accountable without flinching.

He said all the right things. Confident, articulate, well-presented. I hired him.

Within six weeks, it was clear he was struggling. Not with the technical aspects of the role — with the human ones. The difficult conversations weren't happening. The team was drifting. The performance issues he'd been brought in to address were quietly compounding while Mike found reasons to delay.

I sat with him early — not at the end of a quarter, not after the situation had hardened, but within weeks of seeing the pattern. I put a development plan in place. I coached. I gave specific, documented, real-time feedback. I gave him every tool and every opportunity to course-correct.

It wasn't enough. Mike didn't improve. And within his probationary period, I made the decision to let him go.

What followed was a wrongful termination claim — and a painful, expensive, draining process that ultimately settled, not because I had done anything wrong, but because litigation is costly and organizations make pragmatic decisions. It haunted me for a long time. Not because I doubted the call, but because I kept replaying the hiring decision — asking myself what questions I should have asked in that interview that would have told me what I later found out on the job.

What I took from it: do your due diligence at the front end. Probe for evidence of past behaviour, not just confidence in future performance. Ask specifically about the hardest conversations they've had, the performance situations they've navigated, the times they've failed to act and what it cost them. And if you do have to manage someone out, do it with documentation, with consistency, with genuine support offered throughout — and without delay once it's clear the situation isn't going to change.

The lesson isn't to be harder. It's to be earlier, clearer, and more rigorous — both in hiring and in the performance conversations that follow.

> **Do your due diligence at the front end. And when performance conversations are needed — have them early, clearly, and without delay.**

The Toxic Top Performer: A Composite (I Have More of These Than I'd Like)

I'm going to describe a composite here — because I genuinely have more examples to draw from than I'd like to admit, and protecting the innocent (and the guilty) is probably wise at this point in my career.

Picture this: you inherit a team, and within the first two weeks, it becomes clear there is one person everyone either orbits around or avoids. Their numbers are exceptional. Their client relationships are strong. Their manager before you — and the one before that — protected them fiercely because the revenue line was clean and the politics of touching them felt too risky.

But here's what the numbers don't show: three high performers who left in the last 18 months, citing "team culture" as the reason. A pattern of credit-taking so consistent that the people who actually do the work have stopped putting their names on things. Junior team members have learned not to speak in meetings where this person is present. And a quiet, pervasive understanding across the team that there are two sets of rules — one for everyone else, and one for the person who hits their number.

When I inherited situations like this — and I did, more than once — the temptation was always to move carefully. Give it time. Gather more data. Build more trust before touching the third rail. And to a point, that caution is legitimate. You don't walk in on Day One and blow up the revenue engine without understanding what you're dealing with.

But here's what I learned the hard way: every week you delay addressing a toxic top performer is a week your best people are watching to see what you'll do. And every week you don't act is a week they update their answer. By the time you finally have the conversation, the damage to your credibility with the rest of the team is already done — because they've concluded that you either don't see it or you've decided the number is worth more than they are.

The conversation itself doesn't have to be aggressive or punitive. In my experience, the most effective approach is direct, specific, and completely free of ambiguity: here is what I am observing, here is the specific impact it is having on the team and the business, here is what needs to change, and here is the timeline. No softening. No diplomatic cushioning that allows them to walk away thinking it wasn't that serious. And no tolerance for the most common response, which is to perform compliance in your presence while continuing the behaviour everywhere else.

High performance does not buy a licence to harm. That is not a trade-off Whole Human Leadership accepts.

> **Every week you delay addressing a toxic top performer, your best people are watching to see what you'll do. And every week you don't act, they update their answer.**

The Three Lenses of Team Assessment

A complete team assessment looks at every person through three lenses simultaneously. Each one matters. None is sufficient alone.

- What are they actually delivering against the expectations of their role? Not their effort, not their intent, not their potential — their output. Is it meeting the standard? Exceeding it? Falling short? Be specific. Vague assessments of performance lead to vague conversations and no change. **Performance.**

- What is the ceiling of what this person could do with the right development, the right challenge, and the right support? Potential is not the same as performance and confusing the two leads to either under-investing in high performers who haven't yet had the right opportunity or over-promoting people whose current performance doesn't reflect where they could go. **Potential.**

- Does the way this person operates align with the values and behaviours you need in this team? Not personality — behaviour. Not likability — integrity, accountability, how they treat people, how they respond to feedback. A high performer who consistently undermines culture is not an asset. They are a liability with a good quarter attached to it. **Culture fit.**

The interaction between these three lenses is where your most important judgments live. A high performer with low potential and strong culture fit is a different leadership challenge from a low performer with high potential and culture fit issues. The nine-box framework below gives you a structured way to think about all nine combinations — and what each one calls for from you.

What You're Not Allowed to Skip

Both stories above point to the same truth: what you see and don't act on becomes yours. You inherit the history, but you own the future. Phase Two is your window to reset the standard — fairly, transparently, and without drama.

Two patterns consistently get avoided, and both consistently cost new leaders their credibility:

- The revenue is real. So is the damage. What you tolerate, you endorse — and your team is watching to see which matters more to you. **The toxic top performer.**

- The relationship history makes it feel cruel to act. It isn't. What's cruel is leaving someone in a role they're failing at without ever giving them the honest feedback and genuine support to change it. **The long-tenured underperformer.**

In both cases, early is better than late, specific is better than vague, and a difficult conversation handled well is almost always better than a situation left to drift.

The WHL Lens: Performance and Humanity Are Not in Conflict

Whole Human Leadership does not ask you to be soft on performance. It asks you to be honest about it — and to deliver that honesty with care, consistency, and respect for the person on the other side of the conversation.

The Iron Maiden approach to performance management is cold, transactional, and often delayed — because discomfort is managed by avoidance rather than addressed head-on. The Turtle approach is direct, early, and human. It names what is happening clearly, connects it to impact, and creates a genuine path forward — whether that path is development, redirection, or a managed exit.

The leaders who struggle most with team assessment in Phase Two are usually not the ones who are too tough. They are the ones who are too conflict-averse. They soften the feedback until it no longer lands. They delay the conversation until the situation has hardened. They tell themselves they need more data — when what they actually need is more courage.

You already have enough data. You have 30 days of observation, 1:1 conversations, cultural signals, performance indicators, and your own professional instincts. Use them. Have the conversations that need to be had — with compassion, with specificity, and without waiting for the situation to resolve itself. It won't.

> **You already have enough data. What you need now is the courage to use it.**

Having Early Honest Conversations Without Derailing Relationships

The fear most new leaders have about early performance conversations is that they will damage the relationship before trust is fully established. That fear is understandable. It is also, in most cases, backwards.

Done well, an early honest conversation — delivered with clarity, care, and genuine investment in the person's success — is one of the most powerful trust-building acts available to a new leader. It signals that you pay attention, that you tell the truth, and that you are invested enough in this person to have an uncomfortable conversation rather than letting them drift.

What damages relationships is not honesty. It is vagueness, inconsistency, or feedback delivered so late that the person feels ambushed. Lead with specifics, not generalizations. Lead with impact, not character judgments. Lead with a genuine question about what's getting in the way — because in most cases, the person already knows something isn't working. They've just been waiting for someone with authority to say it out loud.

Template: Team Diagnostic — Performance, Potential & Culture Fit

Complete one row per direct report by end of Day 50. Rate Performance and Potential as High / Medium / Low. Rate Culture Fit as Strong / OK / Weak. Your Assessment & Next Step column should include one specific action — a development conversation, a stretch assignment, a performance discussion, or a watch note.

Name / Role	Performance	Potential	Culture Fit	Your Assessment & Next Step
	H / M / L	H / M / L	Strong / OK / Weak	
	H / M / L	H / M / L	Strong / OK / Weak	

	H / M / L	H / M / L	Strong / OK / Weak	
	H / M / L	H / M / L	Strong / OK / Weak	
	H / M / L	H / M / L	Strong / OK / Weak	
	H / M / L	H / M / L	Strong / OK / Weak	
	H / M / L	H / M / L	Strong / OK / Weak	
	H / M / L	H / M / L	Strong / OK / Weak	

Self-Assessment Tool: The Nine-Box — Where Does Each Person Sit?

Map each direct report into the appropriate box based on your Phase Two assessment. Use this to prioritize your leadership energy — your stars need stretching, your low/low need addressing, and everyone in between needs a clear and honest conversation about what comes next.

LOW PERFORMANCE HIGH POTENTIAL	MEDIUM PERFORMANCE HIGH POTENTIAL	HIGH PERFORMANCE HIGH POTENTIAL
Invest with clear expectations. Coach hard or move on. Names:	*Develop and accelerate. These are your future leaders.* Names:	*Your stars. Protect, stretch, and sponsor them.* Names:
LOW PERFORMANCE MEDIUM POTENTIAL	**MEDIUM PERFORMANCE MEDIUM POTENTIAL**	**HIGH PERFORMANCE MEDIUM POTENTIAL**
Manage performance actively. Set a clear timeline. Names:	*Solid contributors. Stabilize and focus.* Names:	*Reliable delivery. Recognize and retain.* Names:
LOW PERFORMANCE LOW POTENTIAL	**MEDIUM PERFORMANCE LOW POTENTIAL**	**HIGH PERFORMANCE LOW POTENTIAL**
Address immediately. This cannot drift. Names:	*Consider role fit. Have the honest conversation.* Names:	*Value what they deliver. Don't over-invest in growth.* Names:

Template: Early Honest Conversations — What to Say and What to Avoid

Use this as a preparation guide before any difficult performance or development conversation in Phase Two. Specificity and care are not opposites — you need both.

Situation	What to Say	What to Avoid
High performer, early signal they may be disengaged	"I've noticed you seem less energized lately. I want to understand what's going on — is there something about this role or environment that isn't working for you?"	*Waiting until the disengagement is visible to everyone else before addressing it.*
Underperformer who has been here a long time	"I want to be honest with you — the output I'm seeing isn't meeting the standard for this role. I want to understand what's getting in the way and figure out together how to change that."	*Softening the feedback so much it doesn't land. They need to hear it clearly.*
Toxic top performer — culture impact is clear	"Your results are strong and I want you to succeed here. I'm also hearing consistent feedback about how you're working with the team that I can't ignore. Here's specifically what I'm seeing…"	*"Everyone says you're difficult but the numbers are great so let's just manage around it."*
High potential who hasn't been challenged or developed	"Based on what I've observed, I think you're capable of significantly more than your current role is asking of you. I'd like to talk about what that could look like."	*Waiting for the right moment. The right moment is now.*

Someone who may not be in the right role	"I want to have an honest conversation about fit. I don't think this role is playing to your strengths — and I'd rather have that conversation now than let it drag."	*Letting them stay in a role they're failing at because the conversation feels risky.*

Before you complete your Phase Two people assessment, sit with these questions. The discomfort they produce is directional — it's pointing you toward the conversations that need to happen.

- Who on your team are you giving the benefit of the doubt — and is that based on evidence or on your reluctance to have a hard conversation?

- Who is the toxic top performer in your team, and what is their real impact on the people around them?

- Who has been in a role too long without honest feedback? What has that cost them — and the team?

- Who is your highest-potential person, and what are you doing to ensure they stay?

- Where is your own bias showing up in this assessment? Whose performance are you rating higher because you like them, and whose are you rating lower because they challenge you?

- Which conversation are you most avoiding? Write down the first sentence you'll use to open it — then schedule it before the end of Phase Two.

Section 2.3 Key Takeaways

- People decisions are the most consequential decisions you will make. Get the assessment right before you get the strategy right.

- Assess through three lenses simultaneously: performance, potential, and culture fit. All three matter. None can substitute for the others.

- What you tolerate, you endorse. The toxic top performer and the long-tenured underperformer are both your responsibility to address in Phase Two.

- The Turtle is direct, early, and human. Performance management is not in conflict with Whole Human Leadership — it is an expression of it.

- Early honest conversations build trust when done with specificity and care. Delayed or softened feedback destroys it.

- You already have enough data. What you need now is the courage to act on it.

Coming Up in Section 2.4: *Navigating Change That Was Already in Motion — what to do when you inherit a transformation, restructure, or crisis mid-stream, and how to lead through uncertainty without becoming the source of more of it.*

SECTION 2.4: NAVIGATING CHANGE THAT WAS ALREADY IN MOTION

Nobody walks into a new leadership role and finds a clean slate. The organization was in motion before you arrived — restructures in progress, transformation initiatives that have lost momentum, decisions already made that you now have to implement, and cultural wounds still healing from the last round of change. Your job is not to pause all of that until you've had time to form your own views. Your job is to understand what's already moving, make an honest assessment of each initiative, and decide quickly where to accelerate, where to intervene, and where to let things run.

That sounds straightforward. It isn't. Inherited change is one of the most politically and emotionally charged environments a new leader can step into — because everyone already has a position, a history, and a stake in the outcome. And many of them are watching closely to see whether you'll have the courage to say what you actually think, or whether you'll manage by consensus and tell everyone what they want to hear.

Your team doesn't need a cheerleader for change that isn't working. They need a leader who will look at what's actually happening, tell the truth about it, and then do something about it. That combination

— honesty plus action — is what builds credibility in a change environment faster than anything else.

> **Your team doesn't need a cheerleader for change that isn't working. They need a leader who will tell the truth about it — and then do something.**

The Story Behind the Framework: When the Division Wins and the Company Loses

Early in my tenure at a large, established organization — the kind with decades of history, a dominant market position, and a culture that had calcified around both — I was brought in to lead a business unit and support the organizational transformation. The business was facing a classic commoditization trap: the core offering that had built the company was under margin pressure, and the path forward required moving upmarket into higher-value, more strategic work. I understood the mandate. I believed in it. And I was prepared to run hard at it.

From the first few months of listening and looking honestly at the organization, I understood that our division could not carry the whole company on its back. I told the senior executive I reported to exactly that: we can grow this business unit, we can transform what we own, and we will. But if the rest of the organization doesn't change alongside us, the overall ambition stalls. You can't build a high-value, strategic business on a foundation that's still operating like it's 2005.

That conversation was heard. It was acknowledged. And then, largely, it was set aside.

So we got to work. A year later, our division had delivered — real growth, real transformation, real movement into exactly the kind of work the company said it wanted to be known for. I was proud of what the team built. And I watched, in real time, as the broader organizational reality I had flagged came to fruition anyway. The legacy thinking that had been protected — the leaders who were comfortable in old ways, the structures built for a business model that was slowly becoming obsolete — created the drag I had anticipated. The CEO was unwilling to make the hard calls on talent and direction that the strategy actually required. The gap between what the company said it wanted to be and what it was willing to become kept widening.

The lesson I took from that experience is not that I should have stayed quiet. I said what I saw, to the right person, at the right level, with data and a clear alternative. That is exactly what a leader is supposed to do. The lesson is that you can be right about the diagnosis and still not be able to change the outcome — because the decisions that would have made the difference weren't yours to make.

When you inherit change that is causing harm, or step into a transformation that is structurally incomplete, your obligation is to say so clearly and to keep saying it through the right channels. What you cannot do is hold yourself responsible for decisions that sit above your authority. You own your sphere. You lead it as well as it can be led.

And when you have done everything in your power to influence the direction, and the direction doesn't change — that is when the work becomes personal. Not just strategic. Personal.

You have to ask yourself some hard questions. Can I continue to lead with integrity inside this environment, or am I compromising myself to stay? Am I still growing here, or am I just managing decline with good manners? What is this costing me — professionally, personally, in terms of who I am as a leader? And perhaps most importantly: what am I modelling for the people on my team who are watching how I navigate this?

There is no universal right answer. Some environments are worth staying in and fighting for, even when the progress is slow and the frustration is real. Others ask you to become a smaller version of yourself just to survive in them — and that is a price no role is worth. The Turtle knows the difference. Not always immediately, and not always easily. But eventually.

I made my decision. And I made it with clarity, because I had been honest with myself all along about what I was seeing, what I was saying, and what was and wasn't changing. That honesty — with your organization and with yourself — is not a soft skill. It is the most important leadership competency you will ever develop.

> **You can be right about the diagnosis and still not be able to change the outcome. Your obligation is to say what you see — and to be honest with yourself about what it means.**

Taking Inventory: What's Already in Flight

Before you can navigate inherited change effectively, you need a complete picture of what's in motion. In Phase One, you were gathering information. By Phase Two, you should be able to map every significant change initiative with clarity: what it is, where it's at, who owns it, what the team impact is, and what your role needs to be.

Most organizations have more change in flight than anyone has formally acknowledged. Some of it is visible — a technology transformation, a restructure, a new go-to-market strategy. Some of it is invisible — cultural change that was quietly initiated by your predecessor, a team rebuild that was never formalized, a strategic pivot that was announced and then never resourced. All of it is yours to navigate.

The change inventory template below gives you a structured way to capture everything in one place. Don't rely on what you've been briefed on. Ask directly of your direct reports, your peers, and the people in the organization who were closest to the work. The unofficial view of what's actually happening with each initiative is almost always more accurate than the official one.

Four Types of Inherited Change — and What Each One Requires

Not all inherited change is the same. The leadership response that works for one type will fail for another. Here are the four situations you're most likely to encounter:

- Some initiatives will be progressing well — quietly, without fanfare, because the people running them are just getting on with it. Your job here is to recognize it, name it, and protect it from the disruption that new leadership often inadvertently creates. Don't fix what isn't broken. Don't rebrand it as yours. Don't add process overhead that slows down something that has momentum. Show up, acknowledge the work, remove the obstacles, and get out of the way. **Change that's working and needs protection.**

- An initiative that was announced with energy and has since gone quiet. The team knows it's not progressing. Leadership may or may not. Your first move is not to push harder — it's to understand why it stalled. Diagnosis before action. Is it a resource problem? A capability problem? A political problem? A problem with the original design? Each answer leads to a different intervention. **Change that's stalled and needs diagnosis.**

- Change that is nominally progressing but is creating damage — to people, to culture, to operational performance — that outweighs whatever benefit it was designed to deliver. This is the hardest situation to navigate as a new leader because the change typically has senior sponsorship and you are being asked to implement it, not question it. Do it anyway. Bring data, bring impact evidence, bring a specific alternative. Say what you see, to the right person, at the right level. You may not always win that argument. But you have to make it. **Change that's causing harm and needs to be challenged.**

- Initiatives that were started, partially implemented, and left in a state of ambiguity. Some should be completed. Some should be formally stopped. Some should be redesigned. The worst outcome is the status quo — leaving the ambiguity unresolved, which forces your team to operate in an environment where nobody knows what the rules are. Make the call. Communicate it clearly. Move on. **Change that's incomplete and needs a decision.**

Leading Through Uncertainty Without Becoming the Source of More of It

The most damaging thing a leader can do in a change environment is add uncertainty to an already uncertain situation. And new leaders do it constantly — not through bad intent, but through a combination of incomplete information, political caution, and the instinct to avoid committing to things they're not yet sure of.

Here is what that looks like from your team's perspective: you ask questions without sharing your views. You consult widely without making decisions. You hedge your language until every statement has a trapdoor. You tell different people different things depending on what they seem to need to hear. And your team, watching all of this, concludes that you either don't know what's going on, don't have the authority to act, or don't trust them enough to be straight with them.

None of those conclusions build credibility. All of them accelerate the disengagement that change environments already generate.

The antidote is not false certainty. You don't have to pretend to have answers you don't have. The antidote is honest, consistent, specific communication — even when what you're communicating is uncertainty. There is a profound difference between a leader who says, "I don't know yet, and here's what I'm doing to find out," and one who says nothing and lets the silence fill with speculation.

Communicate early, often, and in plain language. Share what you know. Be explicit about what you don't know and when you expect to know it. Acknowledge the human impact of the change you're navigating. And when you make a decision — communicate it, explain the reasoning, and move forward without relitigating it every time someone pushes back.

> **There is a profound difference between saying 'I don't know yet, and here's what I'm doing to find out' and saying nothing at all.**

The WHL Lens: Authenticity Under Pressure

Change is where your Whole Human Leadership is tested most directly. It is easy to lead with empathy and authenticity when things are stable. It is harder — and more important — when the environment is uncertain, the decisions are difficult, and the people around you are anxious.

The Turtle navigates change by staying grounded in core values, even when the external environment is in motion. This means being honest when the honest thing is hard. It means acknowledging the emotional weight of what your team is carrying, without letting that acknowledgment become an excuse for inaction. It means making the calls you need to make — decisively, transparently, and with genuine care for the people affected.

It also means knowing when you've reached the limit of what you can influence, and having the courage to either accept that limit or leave. Not every change environment is navigable. Not every organization is willing to hear the truth. The Turtle knows the difference between productive discomfort — the kind that comes from doing hard things well — and an environment that is fundamentally incompatible with leading with integrity. In the first case, you stay and fight. In the second, you turn around.

Template: Change Inventory — What's Already in Motion

List every change initiative, restructure, transformation, or significant decision already in flight when you arrived. Be specific about what stage it's at, what the team impact is, and what your role needs to be. Complete by Day 40.

Change Initiative	Stage	Team Impact	Your Role & Priority Action
*Stage options: Planning	In progress	Stalled	Near completion	Unclear*			

Template: Change Communication Framework

Use this framework to prepare your communication approach for each significant change scenario you face in Phase Two. The principle is always the same: be honest before the rumours are.

Scenario	Principle	What to Say	Common Trap
You don't have answers yet	Say so — explicitly and without apology	*"I don't have the full picture yet. What I can tell you is that I'm working to understand it, and I will share what I know as soon as I can — including the things that are hard to hear."*	Staying silent and letting the rumour mill fill the gap.
The change is going to affect people negatively	Be honest before the rumours are	*"I want to be direct with you. This change is going to affect some roles on this team. I'm committed to being transparent about what I know and when."*	Softening the message so much that people are blindsided when the reality lands.
You disagree with a decision made above you	Align publicly, advocate privately	*"This is the direction we're taking. My job — and yours — is to execute it as well as we can. I'll continue to share my perspective with leadership on how this lands."*	Publicly distancing yourself from decisions you're expected to implement. It erodes your credibility with both directions.

The team is exhausted by the pace of change	Name it. Don't dismiss it.	*"I hear you. The pace has been relentless. I'm not going to pretend otherwise. Here's what I'm doing to manage the load going forward — and here's what I need from you."*	*Motivational language that doesn't acknowledge the real experience. It reads as tone-deaf.*
A change is stalled and no one knows why	Diagnose before you act	*"Before we push harder on this, I want to understand what's actually blocking it. Let's get the right people in a room and be honest about what's going on."*	*Adding urgency to a stalled initiative without understanding the root cause. It creates pressure without progress.*

REFLECTION: WHERE ARE YOU IN THE CHANGE?

Use these questions to position yourself clearly within the change environment you've inherited before you commit to a course of action.

- What is the single most significant change initiative you've inherited — and what is your honest assessment of whether it's working?

- Where are you being asked to implement something you have genuine reservations about? Have you said so to the right person at the right level?

- What change is stalled on your watch? What's actually causing it — and are you addressing that root cause or just adding pressure?

- How are you communicating about change with your team? Are you being specific and honest, or are you hedging in ways that create more uncertainty than they resolve?

- What is the human cost of the change currently in motion? Is your team carrying that weight without acknowledgment?

- Where are you adding uncertainty to an already uncertain environment — and what would it look like to stop?

COMPLETING PHASE TWO

By the end of Day 60, you should be able to say:

- I have an honest, three-layer diagnosis of this business — data, narrative, and observed reality.

- I know where trust is strong, where it needs building, and I have invested deliberately in the relationships that matter most.

- I have assessed every direct report across performance, potential, and culture fit — and I've had, or scheduled, the conversations that needed to happen.

- I understand every significant change initiative in flight — what's working, what's stalled, what's causing harm, and what needs a decision.

- I am communicating with my team honestly, specifically, and consistently — especially about the things I don't yet know.

If you can say yes to all five — you're ready for Phase Three.

Section 2.4 Key Takeaways

- Inherited change is yours to navigate — not pause, not rebrand, and not manage by consensus.

- Take a full inventory of what's in motion before you decide what to do about any of it.

- The four types of inherited change each require a different response: protect, diagnose, challenge, or decide.

- Honest, specific communication reduces uncertainty. Hedging and silence create it.

- The WHL leader is authentic under pressure — acknowledging the human weight of change while continuing to lead through it.

- Know the difference between productive discomfort and an environment incompatible with your values. In the first case, stay and fight. In the second, turn around.

Coming Up in Phase Three: *Days 61–90 — Plan & Commit. With a clear diagnosis and trusted relationships in place, it's time to build your strategy, present your plan, establish your leadership brand, and set your team up to win long after Day 90.*

PLAN & COMMIT

SECTION 3.1: BUILDING YOUR 90-DAY-FORWARD STRATEGY

You have sixty days of information, observation, and relationship-building behind you. You know the business — what it sells, where it struggles, what the numbers say and what they don't. You know the people — who the high performers are, who the blockers are, what's been tolerated for too long and what's been overlooked for even longer. You have a diagnosis. You have a political map. You have the beginnings of trust.

Now you build the plan.

Phase Three is where everything you've gathered becomes something concrete — a clear set of priorities, a credible path forward, and a commitment to your team and your stakeholders about what you're going to do and how you're going to do it. This is not the moment for more analysis. It's the moment for judgment — the distinctly human capacity to take incomplete information, apply your experience and values to it, and make a call.

The leaders who struggle most in Phase Three are not the ones who don't know enough. After 60 days of disciplined listening and assessing, you know enough. The leaders who struggle are the ones who can't move from analysis to commitment — who keep gathering data because committing to a direction feels riskier than staying in a posture of inquiry. It isn't. At Day 60, the cost of continued uncertainty outweighs the cost of an imperfect plan.

> **After 60 days of disciplined listening, you know enough. The cost of continued uncertainty now outweighs the cost of an imperfect plan.**

What a Credible Plan Actually Looks Like

A credible 90-day-forward strategy is not a vision document. It is not a list of aspirations or a set of principles. It is a specific, prioritized, resourced set of commitments — with owners, timelines, and success metrics attached to each one — that your team can hold you accountable to.

The distinction matters. New leaders frequently present plans that sound impressive in a leadership meeting and mean very little on the ground — because the priorities are too broad, the ownership is unclear, the timelines are vague, and there's no honest conversation about what it will actually take to get from here to there. That kind of plan builds neither credibility nor momentum. It builds skepticism.

A credible plan has the following characteristics:

- Every priority should be traceable back to something specific you learned in Phases One and Two. If you can't explain why a priority made the list, it shouldn't be on it. **It is grounded in the diagnosis.**

- Most new leaders try to do too much. The plan that attempts ten priorities will deliver three of them poorly. The plan that commits to five and delivers all of them builds the credibility and momentum that makes the next five possible. Be ruthless about what goes in. **It is focused.**

- Business outcomes and people outcomes are tracked with equal seriousness. Revenue and culture. Performance and engagement. The Turtle does not present a plan that optimizes for one at the expense of the other. **It holds the dual mandate.**

- Not names assigned to items on a slide. People who have been part of the conversation, who understand the priority and the timeline, and who have committed — explicitly — to the outcome. **It has owners who have agreed to own it.**

- A credible plan names the things that are important but are not priorities for this cycle — and explains why. This signals that you've made deliberate choices, not just listed everything and called it strategy. **It acknowledges what it doesn't include.**

The Dual Mandate: People and Business Outcomes Are Not in Competition

One of the most persistent myths in leadership is that people-focused leadership is somehow softer or slower than results-focused leadership. That empathy and accountability are on opposite ends of a spectrum and you have to choose where to sit.

The data — and 30 years of my own experience — say otherwise. Organizations with strong cultures consistently outperform those without. Leaders who invest in their people's development and well-being retain their best performers longer, build higher-performing teams, and deliver more sustainable results. The trade-off is false.

Your 90-day-forward strategy should reflect this. For every business priority, there is a corresponding people reality that either enables or undermines it. A revenue growth target is only achievable if the team driving it is engaged, capable, and in the right roles. A cost reduction initiative will only land cleanly if the people affected are treated with dignity and the communication is honest. An operational transformation will only stick if the culture supports the new ways of working.

The Dual Mandate Dashboard in the tools section below asks you to track both columns simultaneously — people outcomes alongside business outcomes — with the same level of specificity, the same defined metrics, and the same accountability. If your plan doesn't have both, it isn't a whole human strategy. It's half a plan.

> **For every business priority, there is a corresponding people reality that either enables or undermines it. Your plan needs both.**

Prioritizing: The Ruthless Art of Saying No

Strategy is as much about what you won't do as what you will. In the first 90 days, with limited established credibility and a team that is still calibrating their trust in you, the ability to focus is not a luxury — it is a prerequisite for delivering anything meaningful.

The temptation is to put everything on the list. Every problem you've identified, every opportunity you've spotted, every gap you've diagnosed. It feels responsible. It feels thorough. It is neither. A plan that tries to address everything addresses nothing — because the resources, the attention, and the organizational energy required to execute are finite, and spreading them too thin guarantees mediocre outcomes across the board.

The priority filter below gives you a structured way to make the cut. Every proposed priority goes through three tests: does it move the needle on something that genuinely matters, can it realistically be achieved in 90 days with available resources, and does it need to happen before or after something else? Anything that fails any of these tests gets parked — not abandoned, but explicitly deferred to the next planning cycle with a clear explanation of why.

Saying no to good ideas is hard. Saying no to your own ideas is harder. Do it anyway. The ability to focus is one of the most credibility-building signals you can send to a new team — because it tells them that you understand the organization's capacity, you respect their time, and you're committed to delivering what you promise rather than promising everything and delivering fragments.

Sequencing: Getting the Order Right

Even a well-focused plan can fail if the sequencing is wrong. Some priorities depend on others being in place first. Some changes require a certain level of trust before they can land. Some structural decisions need a people conversation before they become operational realities.

The most common sequencing mistakes in a new leader's first plan:

- You don't yet have full confidence in who belongs where. Moving too fast on structure before people decisions are made creates confusion and forces corrections that damage credibility. **Announcing structural changes before the team assessment is complete.**

- Culture change requires people to believe you mean it. If you're still in the trust-building phase, a culture initiative lands as a programme, not a commitment. Build the trust first. **Launching culture initiatives before trust is established.**

- Holding people accountable to standards in a system that doesn't support those standards is unfair and counterproductive. Clarify the model, then set the expectations. **Setting performance expectations before the operating model is clear.**

- No one should hear your plan for the first time in a group setting. The people with the most influence — and the most at stake — should have been consulted before you go broad. Surprises in strategy presentations create resistance, even when the strategy is right. **Communicating the strategy before the key stakeholders have heard it privately.**

The right sequence is almost always: people decisions first, structure second, process third, communication throughout. Trust enables everything else. Build it, then build on it.

Template: 90-Day Forward Strategy Framework

For each priority area, identify your specific priority, who owns it, how you'll measure success, and your target timeline. This becomes the foundation for your Day 90 plan presentation in Section 3.2.

Priority Area	Specific Priority / Goal	Owner	Success Metric	Timeline
Business Performance *What needs to change about how this business delivers results?*				
People & Team *What structural or individual changes are needed to have the right people in the right roles?*				
Culture & Ways of Working *What behaviours need to be reinforced, introduced, or stopped?*				
Client / Customer *What needs to change about how we serve and retain our most important relationships?*				

Process & Operations *What is breaking or inefficient enough to address in the next 90 days?*				
Growth & Innovation *Where is the most credible opportunity to build on what's working?*				
Change in Flight *Which inherited initiatives need acceleration, redesign, or a decision to stop?*				

Template: The Dual Mandate Dashboard — People & Business Outcomes

Your strategy should track both columns with equal seriousness. Business metrics without people metrics is an incomplete picture. For each, define your current baseline and your 90-day target.

PEOPLE OUTCOMES	BUSINESS OUTCOMES
*Metric	Baseline	90-Day Target*	*Metric	Baseline	90-Day Target*
Team engagement / morale	Revenue vs. target
Attrition / retention rate	Margin / cost performance
Performance conversation completion rate	Client retention / satisfaction
Internal promotion rate	Pipeline health
Psychological safety indicators	Operational delivery quality
DEI representation progress	Strategic initiative completion rate

Self-Assessment: The Priority Filter — Is This Actually a Priority?

Run every proposed priority through these three filters before it makes the plan. If it can't pass all three, it's not a priority — it's a preference.

FILTER 1	FILTER 2	FILTER 3
Impact	**Achievability**	**Sequencing**
Does this move the needle on a business or people outcome that genuinely matters?	Can this realistically be done in 90 days with available resources and current trust levels?	Does this need to happen before something else can? Or does something else need to happen first?

If it passes all three filters: it goes in the plan.

If it fails Filter 1: drop it.

If it fails Filter 2: park it for the next planning cycle.

If it fails Filter 3: resequence it — identify what needs to happen first.

REFLECTION: BEFORE YOU FINALIZE THE PLAN

Before you present your strategy to anyone, run it through these questions. They're the ones a good challenger would ask — so ask them yourself first.

- Can you trace every priority directly back to something specific you learned in Phases One and Two?

- Is there anything on this list that's there because you want it to be, rather than because the organization needs it?

- What are you leaving off the list — and have you communicated that explicitly, with a rationale?

- Does the plan hold the dual mandate? Where are the people outcomes for each business priority?

- Have the owners you've assigned actually agreed to own these priorities — or have you assigned names to a slide?

- What does this plan assume about trust and relationships that may not yet be fully in place? What's your mitigation?

- What would need to be true for this plan to fail? Are you addressing those risks?

Section 3.1 Key Takeaways

- At Day 60, you know enough. Move from analysis to commitment — the cost of continued uncertainty now outweighs the cost of an imperfect plan.

- A credible plan is specific, prioritized, owned, and grounded in your diagnosis. Aspiration without accountability is not a strategy.

- The dual mandate is non-negotiable. Business outcomes and people outcomes belong in the same plan, tracked with the same rigour.

- Be ruthless about focus. A plan that tries to do everything delivers nothing. Say no to good ideas so you can say yes to the right ones.

- Get the sequencing right. Trust enables everything else — and most structural and cultural changes require trust to be in place before they can land.

- Consult before you communicate. No one with influence should hear your plan for the first time in a group setting.

Coming Up in Section 3.2: *Presenting Your Plan — how to present a strategy that earns commitment rather than compliance, handle pushback with CT and EI in balance, and model the accountability from the top that you're asking for from everyone else.*

PLAN & COMMIT

SECTION 3.2: PRESENTING YOUR PLAN: LEADING THE ROOM

A strategy that stays in a document is not a strategy. It is a thought experiment. The moment a plan becomes real — the moment it becomes something the organization will actually execute — is when you stand in front of the people who matter and commit to it out loud, in specific terms, with accountability attached.

The Day 90 plan presentation is one of the most important leadership moments of your first year. Done well, it is the event that shifts you from being the new leader who is still figuring things out to being the leader this organization is moving behind. Done poorly, it confirms every reservation anyone had about whether you were ready for this role.

The difference between those two outcomes is rarely the quality of the strategy itself. It is the quality of the presentation — how it's framed, how it's structured, how confidently and honestly it's delivered, and how well you handle the inevitable resistance in the room.

This section prepares you for all of it.

> **The moment a plan becomes real is when you commit to it out loud, in front of the people who matter, with accountability attached.**

The Story Behind the Framework: Be Bold or Go Home

When I sat down with Tim and told him the death-by-a-thousand-cuts approach had to stop, I wasn't presenting a polished strategy document. I was delivering an honest assessment of a situation that everyone around me could see, but nobody with a senior enough voice had been willing to name.

What I had going into that conversation was not a perfect plan. What I had was clarity about the problem, conviction about what needed to change, specific evidence of the damage being done, and the willingness to say it plainly — even knowing it might not be well received.

Tim didn't act. That outcome is its own lesson, which we covered in Section 2.4. But the discipline of walking into that room prepared to be honest, to state what I believed, to ask for what I needed, and to accept whatever came from it — that discipline is what I want you to take into your Day 90 presentation.

Your plan presentation is not a performance. It is not a political exercise. It is a leadership act. The room will read your conviction — or your lack of it — more clearly than they'll read your slides. Show up knowing what you believe, why you believe it, and what you're asking for. Everything else is mechanics.

"Be bold or go home" was the instruction I gave myself before I walked into that meeting with Tim. It is the right instruction for your Day 90 presentation too. Not reckless — bold. There is a difference. Reckless is saying things without evidence. Bold is saying true things clearly, even when it would be easier not to.

> **Your plan presentation is not a performance. It is a leadership act. The room will read your conviction more clearly than they'll read your slides.**

Commitment vs. Compliance: The Difference That Defines Execution

There are two ways a room can leave a strategy presentation. The first is with compliance — people have heard the plan, they understand what's expected, and they will execute it because they have to. The second is with commitment — people have heard the plan, they believe in it, and they will execute it because they want to.

Compliance delivers the minimum. Commitment delivers the maximum. And the difference between them is almost entirely determined by how the plan was presented and how the leader showed up in the room.

Compliance presentations are characterized by: a leader who tells rather than engages, priorities that feel imposed rather than co-created, no genuine space for pushback, and an implicit message that the decision has already been made. The room follows because the hierarchy says so.

Commitment presentations are characterized by: a leader who grounds the plan in what they actually heard from the people in the room, priorities that are clearly connected to real organizational needs, genuine space for challenge and refinement, and an explicit invitation to own the outcome together. The room follows because they believe in where they're going — and because they can see themselves in the plan.

You build commitment by involving people before you present to them. The conversations you've had in the last 60 days — the 1:1s, the listening tours, the trust-building sessions — are not separate from the plan presentation. They are what makes the plan presentation land. People who were consulted will defend a plan they helped shape. People who were surprised will resist a plan they don't recognize.

Modelling Accountability from the Top

One of the most powerful things you can do in a Day 90 plan presentation is model the exact accountability you're asking for from everyone else. This means being specific about what you're committing to personally — not just what the team is committing to, not just what the organization needs to deliver, but what you, as the leader, are holding yourself accountable for.

Name it explicitly. "Here is what I am committing to by Day 180. Here is how you'll know if I'm delivering. Here is what I'm asking you to hold me to." This is not performative vulnerability — it is the practical demonstration that accountability in this team runs in all directions, including up.

Leaders who ask for accountability without modelling it create a culture of compliance at best and cynicism at worst. Leaders who model it — publicly, specifically, with genuine consequences — create a culture where accountability feels like shared ownership rather than top-down surveillance.

The Turtle takes accountability for outcomes, including failures. In your Day 90 presentation, name one thing you got wrong in the first 60 days and what you learned from it. Not a false humility performance — a real example. It will do more to build trust in that room than any slide in your deck.

> **Name one thing you got wrong in the first 60 days and what you learned from it. It will do more for trust than any slide in your deck.**

Handling Pushback: CT and EI in Real Time

Pushback in a plan presentation is not a problem. It is a signal — that people are engaged, that they have a stake in the outcome, and that they trust the environment enough to say what they actually think. A room that nods silently at everything you propose is not a sign of a good plan. It is a sign of a disengaged team or a culture where challenging the leader is not safe.

Welcome the pushback. Prepare for it. And when it comes, resist two instincts that will undermine you: the instinct to defend your position immediately, and the instinct to capitulate entirely to avoid conflict.

The Turtle uses CT to stay grounded in facts and EI to stay connected to the person raising the concern. Every challenge in a plan presentation contains both a logical dimension — is this concern factually valid? — and a human dimension — what is this person actually worried about, and does my response acknowledge that? You need to address both. Answering only the logical dimension leaves people feeling dismissed. Answering only the emotional dimension leaves the plan vulnerable.

The pushback guide below gives you specific CT and EI responses for the six most common forms of resistance you'll encounter. Prepare your version of each before you walk into the room.

Template: Plan Presentation Structure — The Five Sections

Total presentation time: 50 minutes. Always leave 10 minutes for questions. Brief the most influential stakeholders privately before the group presentation — no one with real influence should hear your plan for the first time in a room full of other people.

Section	Time	Purpose	What to Cover	Common Trap
1. What I Heard	**10 min**	Show the room you listened. Ground the plan in the diagnosis.	Summarize the key themes from your Phase One and Two work — business health, people assessment, culture signals, change in flight. Name what's working and what isn't. Be specific. This section builds credibility before you've proposed a single solution.	*Spending too long here. This is context, not the main event.*
2. What I Believe	**10 min**	Establish your judgment and your perspective.	Share your honest assessment of the most important opportunities and risks. This is where you put your stake in the ground — not tentatively, but with the confidence of someone who has spent 60 days earning the right to an opinion. Name the things others may have avoided saying.	*Hedging. If you believe it, say it. Equivocation at this stage reads as lack of conviction.*

3. What I'm Proposing	**15 min**	Present the strategy with clarity, specificity, and ownership.	Walk through your top priorities using the dual mandate framework — business outcomes and people outcomes side by side. For each priority: what, why, who owns it, how you'll measure it, and by when. Make it concrete enough that anyone in the room could hold you accountable to it.	*Too many priorities. If you're presenting more than five to seven, you haven't finished prioritizing.*
4. What I Need	**10 min**	Model accountability and invite partnership.	Be explicit about what you need from this room to deliver the plan — resources, decisions, sponsorship, air cover. New leaders frequently omit this section out of a desire to appear self-sufficient. Don't. Asking for what you need is not weakness. It's the beginning of accountability in both directions.	*Being vague. "Support from leadership" is not a request. Specific asks get specific responses.*

5. How I'll Report Back	5 min	Close the loop on accountability.	Commit to a reporting cadence — how you'll track progress, how you'll communicate it, and what you'll do when something isn't on track. This signals that this plan is not a one-time presentation. It is a living commitment.	*Skipping this entirely. Without a reporting structure, the plan has no accountability infrastructure.*

Template: Handling Pushback — CT and EI in the Room

Prepare for the pushback you're most likely to get before you walk into the room. For each, have both a CT response (the logical, factual answer) and an EI response (the relational, human answer). You'll need both.

Pushback	What It Usually Means	CT Response	EI Response
"That's not how we do things here."	You've touched something that is culturally entrenched — possibly for good reason, possibly not. This is rarely about the specific idea.	*"Help me understand how it has worked historically and what you'd want to protect about that approach."*	*Acknowledge the history. Don't dismiss it. Ask questions before you defend your position.*

"We tried that before and it didn't work."	There is institutional memory — and institutional pain — attached to this idea. The concern is real even if the context has changed.	*"That's useful context. Can you tell me more about what happened — specifically what the conditions were and what broke down?"*	*Validate the experience. Separate the past failure from the current proposal without dismissing their concern.*
"The timeline is too aggressive."	Either the timeline genuinely is unrealistic, or there is resistance to the change itself being expressed through the timeline.	*"What specifically concerns you about the timeline? Let's look at the dependencies and see if there's a constraint I haven't accounted for."*	*Take this seriously — don't defend the timeline reflexively. There may be real information here.*
"Leadership won't support this."	Political warning — possibly accurate, possibly a deflection. Either way, it's telling you something about the landscape.	*"Who specifically do you think would push back, and what would their concern be? I want to make sure I've addressed it."*	*Don't get defensive. This is useful intelligence. Use it to refine your stakeholder strategy.*

"We don't have the resources to do this."	Could be a legitimate constraint. Could also be organizational learned helplessness — the habit of citing resources to avoid commitment.	*"Let's get specific. What resources are needed, what do we currently have, and what's the gap? I'd rather solve a real constraint than assume it's insurmountable."*	*Treat this as a problem to solve together, not a challenge to your plan.*
Silence — no one responds at all.	Often the most dangerous response. Could mean agreement, could mean disengagement, could mean the room has already decided something they're not saying to your face.	*Name it directly: "I'm not getting much reaction — I'd rather hear the honest pushback now than find out later that there were concerns I didn't know about."*	*Read the room. Who is exchanging looks? Who is notably quiet? Those are the conversations to have privately after the meeting.*

Action Planning Page: Plan Presentation Prep Checklist

Work through this checklist before, during, and after your Day 90 plan presentation. The items are sequenced deliberately — the before-meeting preparation determines whether the in-room conversation is productive.

	BEFORE THE MEETING
☐	Briefed every high-influence stakeholder privately — no surprises in the room
☐	Confirmed the plan has been reviewed by at least two people who will push back honestly
☐	Prepared specific asks — not "support" but named decisions, resources, and sponsorship
☐	Rehearsed the opening two minutes — how you frame the purpose of the presentation matters
☐	Anticipated the three most likely objections and prepared both a CT and EI response for each

	IN THE ROOM
☐	Opened by referencing what you heard — the diagnosis before the prescription
☐	Stated your priorities specifically — no vague goals, no undefined success metrics
☐	Named what's not in the plan and why — deliberate exclusion signals disciplined thinking
☐	Asked explicitly for what you need — resources, decisions, air cover
☐	Created space for genuine pushback — invited dissent rather than consensus performance
☐	Committed to a specific reporting cadence — closed the accountability loop

AFTER THE MEETING	
☐	Followed up with anyone who was notably quiet or who raised concerns not fully resolved
☐	Sent a written summary of commitments within 48 hours — yours and theirs
☐	Scheduled the first progress check-in before leaving the room
☐	Noted any pushback that revealed political dynamics worth tracking

REFLECTION: YOUR LEADERSHIP VOICE IN THE ROOM

The quality of your Day 90 presentation will be determined less by the content of the slides and more by how you show up. These questions prepare you for that.

- What is the one thing you most need this room to believe about you as a leader after this presentation? Are you preparing to demonstrate it?

- What is the thing you're most tempted to soften or omit — and what would it cost to say it plainly?

- Who in this room is most likely to push back? Have you had a private conversation with them before the meeting?

- What will you acknowledge getting wrong in the first 60 days — and how will you frame it as learning, not apology?

- What are you asking the room to hold you personally accountable to? Have you made that explicit in your plan?

- What does commitment look like in this room — and how will you know by the end of the presentation whether you've achieved it or just compliance?

Section 3.2 Key Takeaways

- Your Day 90 plan presentation is a leadership act, not a reporting exercise. Show up with conviction, honesty, and accountability.

- Structure matters: What I Heard → What I Believe → What I'm Proposing → What I Need → How I'll Report Back.

- Brief high-influence stakeholders privately before the group presentation. No one with real influence should be surprised in a room full of people.

- The goal is commitment, not compliance. Build it by involving people before you present to them.

- Model the accountability you're asking for — name what you're personally committing to and what you got wrong in the first 60 days.

- Welcome pushback. Prepare for the six most common forms. Use CT to address the logic and EI to address the person.

Coming Up in Section 3.3: *Establishing Your Leadership Brand — what your team now believes about who you are as a leader, how to define and live your personalized Whole Human Leadership style, and how to build the presence that sustains long after Day 90.*

SECTION 3.3: ESTABLISHING YOUR LEADERSHIP BRAND

Whether you've been deliberate about it or not, by Day 90 you have a leadership brand in this organization. Your team has formed an opinion about who you are, how you lead, and what it's like to work for you. Your stakeholders have formed a view about whether you can be trusted, whether you deliver, and whether you're the kind of leader they want to invest in. Your peers have formed a sense of whether you're someone worth knowing or someone worth managing around.

The question is not whether you have a brand. You do. The question is whether the brand you've built in the first 90 days is the one you intended — and whether it reflects the Whole Human Leader you're committed to becoming.

This section is about taking stock of that, with honest eyes, and then defining — deliberately and in your own voice — the leadership identity you're going to carry forward from here.

> **The question is not whether you have a brand. You do. The question is whether it's the one you intended.**

The Story Behind the Framework: Mary

I once coached a woman I'll call Mary who was exceptional with clients. She walked into rooms and elevated them — solutions-focused, warm, energetic. Her instincts were sharp, her relationships were strong, and the people who worked with her loved her.

What was holding Mary back wasn't capability. It was the story she was telling about herself — and the one she was allowing others to tell. She didn't have a college degree, and rather than leading with everything she did have, she led with that absence. She mentioned it in meetings, in client presentations, in her own 1:1s with me. She had been told early in her career that her lack of formal education would limit her advancement, and she'd been carrying that in a heavy backpack ever since.

The other thing holding her back was how she showed up physically. She dressed for a different kind of room than the one she was trying to enter. Not because her personal style was wrong — but because she hadn't yet understood that the way you present yourself in a professional context is one of the signals your audience uses to calibrate their expectations of you. Context matters. You can be fully yourself and still adapt your expression of that self to the environment you're operating in.

What I worked with Mary on over several years was not a rebrand. It was a reclamation. I helped her unpack the heavy backpack — the stories about what she lacked — and replace them with a clear-eyed account of what she actually had. I helped her develop her professional presence not by changing who she was, but by bringing more of who she actually was into the room.

The last I heard, Mary had advanced significantly in her career. Not because she had acquired a degree. Because she had found her voice, owned her strengths, and stopped apologizing for the parts of herself that made her different.

Your leadership brand is not what's on your CV. It is not the polished version of yourself you perform in high-stakes meetings. It is the full expression of your values, your experience, your character, and your way of being in the world — brought deliberately and consistently into your professional life. That is what Whole Human Leadership asks of you. And that is what the most enduring leadership brands are built from.

> **Your leadership brand is not what's on your CV. It is the full expression of your values, your character, and your way of being — brought deliberately into your professional life.**

Executive Presence vs. Whole Human Leadership: The Inside-Out Difference

Executive Presence is a well-established concept in leadership development, and it's worth engaging with directly — because it's almost certainly something you've been told you need, and it's genuinely useful up to a point.

The classic definition of Executive Presence, as articulated by author Sylvia Ann Hewlett, rests on three pillars: gravitas (how you act), communication (how you speak), and appearance (how you look). There is real value in each of these. How you carry yourself, how you communicate, and how you present yourself are all signals your audience reads — consciously and unconsciously — and they do affect how you're perceived.

The limitation of Executive Presence, as traditionally conceived, is that it starts on the outside. It asks you to project an image — to perform a version of leadership that your audience will find credible and compelling. At its worst, it becomes a set of rules about how to act, speak, and look that are based on historical models of leadership — models that were predominantly male, predominantly hierarchical, and predominantly about projecting authority rather than building trust.

Whole Human Leadership starts on the inside. It asks you not to perform leadership but to be it — from a foundation of self-awareness, core values, and genuine human connection. The presence that results is not a projection. It is a natural expression of someone who knows who they are, why they lead, and what they stand for.

The comparison table below maps the key differences. Use it not to dismiss Executive Presence — which has genuine value — but to ensure that whatever presence you're building is grounded in the inside-out approach that makes it authentic rather than performed.

Executive Presence vs. Whole Human Leadership: Inside Out

Executive Presence is a useful concept — but it is incomplete without WHL. The legacy version asks you to perform leadership. Whole Human Leadership asks you to be it. As you define your leadership brand, use this table to ensure you're building from the inside out.

Dimension	Legacy Executive Presence	Whole Human Leadership
Source	*External — how you act, speak, and look for others*	Internal — who you are, what you value, how you lead from the inside out
Goal	*Project an image that attracts followership*	Build relationships that earn followership through trust and authenticity
Gravitas	*Commanding presence through authority and status*	Quiet confidence grounded in self-awareness and conviction
Communication	*How you speak — polish, delivery, authority*	Where you speak from — honesty, empathy, clarity of purpose
Appearance	*How you look — dress, posture, physical presence*	The energy you project — the confidence that comes from being genuinely yourself
Authenticity	*A performance of authenticity for professional contexts*	Authenticity as the baseline — consistent across contexts, not a mask you wear at work
Vulnerability	*Avoided — seen as a liability to credibility*	Used strategically — a trust-building asset when shared with intention
Result	*Compliance — people follow because of the role*	Commitment — people follow because of the person

The Four Elements of a Personal Brand — and Why They Matter Right Now

Your leadership brand is not just a feeling people have about you. It is the sum of four distinct and interconnected elements, each of which you are either building deliberately or leaving to chance. In my book Influence Unleashed: Forging a Lasting Legacy Through Personal Branding, I lay out the full framework for building a brand that lasts. I am going to give you the version that matters most at the 90-day mark — because a new role is one of the highest-leverage moments you will ever have to establish or reset how you are perceived.

The four elements are:

- **What You Do** — Your expertise, credentials, and the specific value you bring to this role. This is your credibility foundation. In a new organization, people are asking: does this person know what they are doing? Your subject matter expertise and track record answer that question. But expertise alone does not build a brand — it just gets you in the room.

- **Who You Are** — Your values, your character, your lived experiences, and your way of being in the world. This is where brand differentiation actually lives. There are plenty of competent people in every organization. There is only one you. The leader who brings their whole human self to work — who has a clear Why, who shares relevant personal context, who leads with both head and heart — is the one people remember, follow, and trust.

- **Your Unique Value Proposition** — The specific combination of what you do and who you are that makes your contribution to this organization distinctively yours. Not just your skills. Not just your personality. The intersection of both — the thing that, when someone asks why they should work for you, follow you, or invest in you, produces a clear and compelling answer. In a new role, your UVP is what separates you from the leader who came before you and the others who were considered for this role.

- **Your Legacy and Impact** — The longer-term mark you intend to leave. What will this team, this organization, or this industry look like because you were here? In the first 90 days, this might feel premature — but it isn't. How you show up today is the first chapter of the legacy you're building. The leaders who have the clearest sense of the impact they want to make are the ones who make the most deliberate choices about how they spend their time, their energy, and their influence.

> **There are plenty of competent people in every organization. There is only one you. Brand is what makes that difference visible.**

Your Personal Brand in a New Role: The Influence Unleashed Connection

A new role is not the time to park your personal brand at the door and blend in until you figure out the culture. It is one of the most important moments to be intentional about it — because the perceptions people form about you in the first 90 days are remarkably sticky. They shape how your ideas are received, whether people seek you out or manage around you, and what kind of followership you build.

The Three Acts of Engagement from Influence Unleashed — Courage, Vulnerability, and Authenticity — are not just brand-building tools for a LinkedIn audience. They are exactly the behaviours that build trust inside an organization in a new leadership role:

- Saying the true thing clearly, even when it's uncomfortable. Having the difficult performance conversation early. Naming the problem in the room that everyone else is stepping around. Presenting your plan with conviction rather than hedging. In a new role, courage is what signals to your team that you are a real leader, not a political operator. **Courage.**

- Acknowledging what you don't know yet without losing your authority. Sharing a relevant moment of failure or learning that builds connection. Admitting publicly when you got something wrong in the first 60 days. Vulnerability is not weakness — it is the specific behaviour that makes trust possible. It is what turns a competent new leader into one people actually want to follow. **Vulnerability.**

- Showing up as the same person in the boardroom, the 1:1, and the all-hands. Letting your values drive your decisions rather than performing the values your new organization says it holds. Being consistent enough that your team can predict how you'll behave — not because you're rigid, but because you're grounded. Authenticity is what makes a leadership brand durable. Everything else is just optics. **Authenticity.**

Your Why — the purpose that drives why you lead the way you lead — is what makes these three acts feel natural rather than performed. When you know your Why, courage is easier because you're acting in service of something that matters to you. Vulnerability is less frightening because you're not protecting an image — you're expressing a truth. And authenticity is not an effort; it is simply what happens when who you are and how you act are aligned.

If you haven't done the deeper work of defining your Why, your Identity, your UVP, and your Legacy — the full Influence Unleashed framework — I'd encourage you to pick up that book and the companion workbook alongside this guide. The brand work and the leadership work are not separate exercises. They are the same exercise. The leader who has done both will show up in their new role with a clarity and presence that no amount of preparation or political savvy can replicate.

> **The brand work and the leadership work are not separate exercises. They are the same exercise.**

What Your Brand Currently Says — and What You Want It to Say

By Day 90, your leadership brand in this organization is already a fact. The question is whether it's accurate — whether what people believe about you reflects who you actually are and how you actually lead.

There are four things worth auditing honestly at this point:

- Not the official feedback — the version they'd give a trusted colleague. Are they energized? Do they feel seen? Do they know where they stand? Do they trust that you'll back them up? This is your culture footprint. **What your team says about working for you.**

- Do they bring you into things early, or manage around you? Do they see you as a collaborator or a competitor? Do they trust your judgment? This is your organizational credibility. **What your peers say about working with you.**

- Not just whether you're delivering — whether you're delivering in a way that builds confidence for the next mandate. Are you managing up effectively, or is your stakeholder relationship transactional? **What your boss sees.**

- This is the most important audit of the four. Does the leader you see in the mirror match the Whole Human Leader you set out to be? Where are the gaps? What do they cost you — and your team? **What you see, when you're honest with yourself.**

The WHL Progress Check below gives you a structured way to revisit your Day 1 Baseline from Section 1.3 and measure genuine movement. Be honest. The point is not to feel good about Day 90. It's to know clearly where you are so you can continue developing beyond it.

Defining Your Personalized WHL Leadership Style

No two Turtles are alike. The Whole Human Leadership framework gives you a structure — but how you express it is entirely your own. The Private Workshop below synthesizes everything from Phases One, Two, and Three into a clear, written statement of who you are as a leader and what you're committing to.

As you work through it, draw on all four elements of your personal brand — your expertise, your identity, your UVP, and the legacy you're building. If you want to go deeper on any of these, the full framework and companion workbook in Influence Unleashed will take you there. This workshop is where the leadership work and the brand work meet.

Your Private Workshop: Defining Your Whole Human Leadership Brand

Work through each prompt honestly. This is not a performance exercise — it's a clarity exercise. You'll use what you develop here in your Day 90 WHL Progress Check and carry it into Section 3.4.

Prompt	Guidance	Your Answer
My leadership moniker	*What word or phrase captures how you want to be known? Not a job title — a leadership identity. Victoria's are the Turnaround Queen and CEO Whisperer. What's yours?*	
My core values (top 3–5)	*The values you would hold even when it's costly to hold them. Not aspirations — operating principles.*	
What I want to be known for	*If someone who worked for you for two years described your leadership style, what would you want them to say?*	

What I bring that's distinctive	*The combination of experience, perspective, and character that no one else on this leadership team brings in quite the same way.*	
Where I'm still developing	*The one or two areas from your WHL Baseline (Section 1.3) that are your most important growth edges. Naming these is not weakness — it's self-awareness.*	
How I want my team to feel	*Not the outputs you want to deliver — the human experience of being on your team. Safe? Challenged? Seen? Held accountable? All of the above?*	
My leadership statement (draft)	*"I, [Name], am a [Moniker], committed to [action] by [value] in [environment]. My purpose is to [outcome] for [people] by [approach]." Write the first honest version.*	

Self-Assessment: WHL Progress Check — Day 90

Revisit your Day 1 WHL Baseline from Section 1.3. Rate yourself on the same traits — honestly, not aspirationally. In the Movement column, note whether you've improved (↑), stayed the same (→), or slipped (↓). Where you slipped: what happened?

WHL Trait / Behaviour	Rarely	Sometimes	Consistently	Movement
I listen more than I talk in new situations	☐	☐	☐	↑ → ↓
I regulate my emotions before responding under pressure	☐	☐	☐	↑ → ↓
I ask open-ended questions before forming conclusions	☐	☐	☐	↑ → ↓
I acknowledge what I don't know without losing credibility	☐	☐	☐	↑ → ↓
I invest time in people regardless of their level or title	☐	☐	☐	↑ → ↓
I create space for others to disagree with me	☐	☐	☐	↑ → ↓
I take accountability for team outcomes — including failures	☐	☐	☐	↑ → ↓

I lead with my values, even when it's uncomfortable	☐	☐	☐	↑ → ↓
I adapt my communication style to the person I'm talking to	☐	☐	☐	↑ → ↓
I recognize and actively work against my own biases	☐	☐	☐	↑ → ↓
I bring my whole self to work — not just my professional shell	☐	☐	☐	↑ → ↓
I build trust before I build change	☐	☐	☐	↑ → ↓

Compare this to your Day 1 Baseline. Where you've moved consistently: those are your strengths to build on. Where you've stayed the same or slipped: those are your development priorities going into Day 91 and beyond. Neither outcome is a verdict. Both are data.

REFLECTION: THE LEADER YOU'RE BECOMING

You've done 90 days of disciplined, intentional work. Before you close this phase and look forward, sit with these questions.

- What is the most important thing you've learned about yourself as a leader in the last 90 days?

- What's one moment from the last 90 days that you're genuinely proud of — and what does it tell you about the leader you're becoming?

- What's one moment you'd do differently — and what would the Turtle have done instead?

- Who on your team has grown in the last 90 days, and how much of that is because of how you've led them?

- If your team described your leadership brand today, what would they say? Is that the brand you want?

- What is the one commitment you're making to yourself about how you'll lead in the next 90 days that you weren't making 90 days ago?

Section 3.3 Key Takeaways

- By Day 90 you have a leadership brand whether you built it deliberately or not. This section is about making it intentional.

- Executive Presence has genuine value — but it starts on the outside. Whole Human Leadership starts on the inside and builds presence from authenticity, not performance.

- Your leadership brand is the full expression of your values, your character, and your way of being — brought consistently into your professional context.

- Audit honestly: what your team, peers, and boss see, and what you see when you're straight with yourself. The gaps between those views are your most important development data.

- Your personalized WHL style is yours alone. The framework is shared. The expression is specific to who you are.

- Write the leadership statement. It is a personal contract — with yourself first, and with your team second.

Coming Up in Section 3.4: *Building a High-Performing Team for the Long Game — turning your team assessment into a development and retention plan, creating accountability without surveillance, and setting the conditions for your team to outperform long after Day 90.*

SECTION 3.4: BUILDING A HIGH-PERFORMING TEAM FOR THE LONG GAME

Everything in this guide has been building to this. The listening, the diagnosing, the trust-building, the plan — all of it is scaffolding. The structure you're building inside that scaffolding is a team that performs not because of how closely you watch them, but because of how deeply they care about the outcome.

That is the Long Game of Leadership. And it starts now — not after Day 90, not once you've fully settled in, not when the organization has stabilized. The conditions you create in your first 90 days determine whether your team is still performing at a high level when you're not in the room. That is the only test of leadership that actually matters.

This section is about turning everything you've learned and built in Phases One, Two, and Three into a sustainable team architecture — one grounded in development, accountability, retention, and the kind of psychological safety that lets people bring their best work to a problem without fear of what happens if it isn't perfect.

> **The only test of leadership that actually matters: is your team still performing at a high level when you're not in the room?**

The Story Behind the Framework: Roger

When I was leading a large Americas business unit, I met Roger at a team gathering — one of those in-person events where you finally get to meet the people you've been leading on screens. I knew within minutes of meeting him that he was exceptional. Not because of anything he said about himself, but because of how he made everyone around him feel.

Roger led an all-female direct report team. Within months of my arrival, every single one of them had independently reached out to me to tell me what kind of leader he was — how he advocated for them, how he invested in their development, how he made them feel seen and capable of more than they'd been asked for. In 20 years of leadership, I have never had an entire team independently advocate for their leader like that. It told me everything I needed to know.

He had ambitions — he wanted to make partner. And the truth was that his financial metrics, in a challenging economic environment, weren't quite where the firm's traditional promotion criteria required. A lesser leader, or a more politically cautious one, would have waited.

I didn't wait. I made it my mission to create the platform for Roger's success. I got him into leadership development programs, placed him on high-visibility projects, and advocated for him at every level. When I resigned before his promotion was finalized, I recorded a video testimonial for the selection committee so my advocacy would survive my departure.

When he called to tell me he'd made partner, what I felt wasn't pride in my own contribution. What I felt was the satisfaction of having helped someone realize their potential — of having used my platform, my relationships, and my seniority in service of someone else's future. That is humble success. That is what the Long Game looks like.

Roger's story is also a reminder that building a high-performing team is not just about managing performance. It is about seeing people — really seeing them — and then using everything available to you to help them become more than they were when you found them. The Turtle doesn't build a team by accident. It builds one with intention, consistency, and genuine care for each person in it.

> **Building a high-performing team is not just about managing performance. It is about seeing people — and then using everything you have to help them become more than they were when you found them.**

From Assessment to Development: Turning the Nine-Box into a Plan

In Section 2.3 you assessed your team. By now you have a nine-box view — who your high performers are, where the potential is, where the culture fit issues live, and where the conversations still need to happen. That assessment is worth nothing if it stays in a document.

Phase Three is where assessment becomes action. Specifically, it becomes a development plan — individual by individual — that answers four questions for every person on your team:

- Most leaders are better at identifying gaps than strengths. The people who stay and grow in your team are usually the ones who feel their best capabilities are being used and developed, not the ones who are only ever being corrected. **What is their greatest strength, and am I actively building on it?**

- Development without communication is invisible. Your team members need to know that you see their potential, you've thought about their growth, and you have a specific commitment to helping them get there. A 1:1 conversation where you say 'here's what I see in you and here's where I think you can go' is one of the highest-value uses of your time as a leader. **What is their most important development priority, and do they know I'm invested in it?**

- Not a vague aspiration. A specific action — a programme, a project, an introduction, a conversation with a more senior leader, a stretch assignment. What will you do, concretely, that you weren't doing before? Write it down. They deserve to know. **What is my specific commitment to them?**

- Development without a milestone is an intention, not a plan. Set a specific, achievable marker that tells you and the team member whether the investment is working. **What does success look like in the next 90 days?**

Accountability Without Surveillance

High-performing teams don't perform because they're being watched. They perform because they own the outcome. Accountability, in its healthiest form, is not a monitoring system imposed from above. It is a culture that the team holds together — where people care enough about the standard to hold themselves to it, and care enough about their colleagues to hold each other to it.

Building that culture in the first 90 days requires the leader to model it before asking for it. Revisiting the LinkedIn comment example from the introduction to this guide: trust doesn't erase accountability — it makes accountability land harder. When people feel trusted, a miss is personal. It matters to them in a way it never would under surveillance. That is the dynamic you are building toward.

The starting point is always the same: set the standard publicly, hold yourself to it first, and address misses early. Everything else follows from those three things. The accountability framework below gives you five specific practices to implement in your first 30 days post-plan presentation.

Psychological Safety: The Non-Negotiable Foundation

No team will perform at its highest level in an environment where people don't feel safe to speak up, raise problems, admit mistakes, or challenge the prevailing view. Psychological safety — the belief that you will not be punished or humiliated for taking an interpersonal risk — is not a nice-to-have. It is the operating condition that determines whether you get your team's best thinking or a carefully managed version of it.

New leaders frequently underestimate how much their own behaviour determines the psychological safety of their team. Every time you respond to bad news with blame rather than curiosity, every time you shut down a dissenting view in a meeting, every time you visibly favour the people who agree with you over the people who challenge you — you are sending a signal. And your team receives that signal clearly, even when you don't intend it.

Building psychological safety is not complicated. It requires four things, practiced consistently:

- When something goes wrong, your first question should be 'help me understand what happened' — not 'who is responsible for this.' One creates problem-solving. The other creates self-protection. **Respond to problems with curiosity, not judgment.**

- The team member who flags an issue before it becomes a crisis is doing you an enormous service. Make sure they know it. Publicly. If you punish the messenger even once, it will take months to undo. **Reward people who surface problems early.**

- Say 'I don't know' when you don't know. Say 'I was wrong' when you were wrong. Say 'that's a better idea than mine' when it is. These are not signs of weakness — they are the signals that it is safe to think out loud in this team. **Model intellectual humility.**

- The difference between a team that innovates and one that doesn't is almost entirely determined by what happens when someone tries something new and it fails. If the consequence is public criticism or career risk, the team will stop trying. If the consequence is a thoughtful debrief and an encouragement to try again, the team will keep going. **Protect people who take risks that don't work out.**

Psychological safety is not a nice-to-have. It is the operating condition that determines whether you get your team's best thinking — or a carefully managed version of it.

Retention: Keeping the People Worth Keeping

High performers don't announce they're leaving. They signal it — weeks, sometimes months, in advance — through changes in energy, engagement, and behaviour that are visible to a leader who is paying attention. Most leaders aren't paying attention at the right level. They're managing the work, not reading the people.

The cost of losing a high performer is significant — typically 1.5 to 2 times their annual salary when you account for recruitment, onboarding, and the productivity loss during transition. But the more important cost is the one that doesn't show up on a spreadsheet: the institutional knowledge, the client relationships, the team culture, and the signal it sends to everyone else about whether this is a place worth staying.

Retention is not primarily a compensation issue, though compensation matters. It is primarily a leadership issue. The research is consistent: people leave managers, not companies. And the factors that drive high performers to stay are almost entirely within your control — clarity about their future, investment in their development, genuine recognition of their contribution, and a leader who advocates for them rather than just managing them.

The retention early warning system below gives you the signals to watch for and the immediate actions to take. The rule of thumb: by the time you're certain someone is thinking about leaving, you're probably already too late. Act on early signals, not confirmed ones.

Sponsorship vs. Mentorship: The Distinction That Changes Careers

Mentorship is advice. Sponsorship is action. Both matter — but they are not the same thing, and conflating them is one of the most common ways well-intentioned leaders underdeliver on their development commitments.

A mentor shares wisdom, provides guidance, and offers perspective. It is a valuable relationship, and if you are someone who can offer mentorship to your team, offer it.

A sponsor uses their platform, their relationships, and their credibility to create opportunities for someone else. They put their name on the line. They say, in a room the person isn't in: 'This person is ready for the next level, and I'm willing to back that.' Roger didn't just need my advice — he needed my advocacy in rooms he couldn't enter. That is sponsorship.

As a new leader, you are building your platform. You don't yet have the full organizational currency to sponsor at scale. But you can begin. Identify the one or two people on your team who have the capability, the character, and the ambition to go further — and make a deliberate commitment to be the leader who helps them get there. Get them in front of the right people. Advocate for them in the right conversations. Create the visibility that their talent deserves but that they can't yet create for themselves.

This is the work that defines your legacy as a leader. Not the strategy you built. Not the plan you presented. The people who became more because of how you led them.

Template: Team Development Plan — Individual by Individual

Complete one row per direct report. This plan bridges your Phase Two people assessment into concrete Day 91+ development and retention commitments. It is a living document — revisit it quarterly.

Name / Role	Top Strength to Build On	Development Priority	My Commitment to Them	90-Day Milestone

Template: Accountability Without Surveillance — Five Practices

Accountability in a high-performing team is not a monitoring system. It is a culture — one where people hold themselves and each other to a standard because they own the outcome. These five practices build that culture.

Practice	What It Means	How to Do It	Common Trap
Set the standard publicly	Name the behaviours and outcomes you expect — clearly, specifically, and for everyone. Standards that live only in your head cannot be held.	*In your first team meeting post-plan presentation, name the three to five non-negotiable standards you're holding yourself and the team to. Write them down. Refer back to them.*	Setting vague standards ('I expect excellence') that are impossible to hold anyone accountable to.
Model it from the top first	Before you hold anyone else accountable, demonstrate the standard yourself — visibly and consistently. Your team is watching whether you hold yourself to what you ask of them.	*When you miss a commitment or get something wrong, name it publicly in the team context. 'I said I'd have this to you by Friday and I didn't. Here's what happened and here's my plan.'*	Applying standards to the team that you exempt yourself from. Nothing destroys accountability culture faster.

Address misses early and specifically	The moment a standard is missed without consequence, it is no longer a standard. It is a suggestion. Address misses quickly, directly, and without drama.	*Within 48 hours of a missed commitment or behaviour, have a private conversation: 'I noticed X. That's not the standard I set. Help me understand what happened and what will be different.'*	*Letting misses accumulate until a performance conversation feels justified. By then, the damage is already done.*
Separate accountability from blame	Accountability is about outcomes and behaviour, not character. The goal is to solve the problem and prevent recurrence — not to assign fault.	*Lead with curiosity, not judgment. 'What got in the way?' before 'Why didn't you?' One opens a problem-solving conversation. The other opens a defensive one.*	*Accountability conversations that feel punitive. They create compliance, not ownership.*

Recognize accountability when you see it	Accountability runs in both directions. When someone owns a miss, acknowledges a problem, or holds themselves to a standard without being asked — name it and celebrate it.	*In team settings: 'I want to acknowledge what [name] did this week — they caught a problem early, flagged it immediately, and came with a solution. That's the standard.'*	*Only noticing accountability when it's absent. Recognition reinforces the culture you're trying to build.*

Template: Retention Early Warning System

Most high performers don't announce they're leaving. They signal it — often weeks or months in advance. This table gives you the signals to watch for and the immediate action to take. Don't wait for certainty before you act.

Early Warning Signal	Risk Level	Immediate Action
Declining energy or enthusiasm in 1:1s	**High**	Have a direct conversation: 'I've noticed a shift in your energy lately. What's going on?' Don't wait for the exit interview.
Reduced initiative — doing the minimum, not suggesting ideas	**Medium– High**	Explore whether the role is still challenging enough. Consider a stretch assignment or expanded responsibility.

Increased complaints about process, culture, or leadership	**Medium**	Take the complaints seriously. They are often a test — is this leader listening? Respond with action, not just acknowledgment.
Withdrawal from team interactions — less visible, less vocal	**Medium–High**	Check in privately. Sometimes withdrawal is workload. Sometimes it's something more serious. You won't know until you ask.
Sudden improvement in presentation and external visibility	**High**	They may be building a job-search profile. Have an open conversation about their career goals and what this organization can offer them.
Asking questions about career paths and advancement timelines	**Medium**	This is a gift — they're telling you what they need. Have a specific conversation about the path, the timeline, and your advocacy.
Peer mentions they seem unhappy or have said something concerning	**High**	Act on this immediately. By the time a peer tells you, the person has already mentally started to leave.

REFLECTION: THE TEAM YOU'RE BUILDING

Before Day 90 closes, sit with these questions about the team you're leaving Phase Three with — and the one you're committed to building beyond it.

- Who on your team is becoming more because of how you've led them in the last 90 days? What specifically did you do that made that possible?

- Who are you sponsoring — not just mentoring — and what concrete actions have you taken on their behalf in a room they weren't in?

- Where is your accountability culture weakest right now? What one practice from the framework above would change it most?

- Who are you most at risk of losing — and have you had a direct, honest conversation with them about what would make them stay?

- What does psychological safety feel like on your team right now? Would your team members say it is safe to raise a problem, admit a mistake, or challenge your thinking?

- In five years, when someone asks a person who worked for you during this period what kind of leader you were — what do you want them to say? Are you building toward that answer right now?

COMPLETING PHASE THREE

By the end of Day 90, you should be able to say:

- I have a credible, specific, prioritized strategy that holds both people and business outcomes — and I've presented it with conviction.

- I have a development plan for every direct report that names my specific commitment to their growth.

- I have established a clear accountability standard, modelled it myself, and addressed the first misses without drama.

- I know who my high-retention risks are and I have acted on the early signals.

- I have defined my leadership brand — my WHL style, my Why, my UVP — and I am living it consistently.

If you can say yes to all five — you've completed the first 90 days. Now the real work begins.

Section 3.4 Key Takeaways

- The Long Game test: is your team performing at a high level when you're not in the room? If yes, you're building something sustainable.

- Turn your nine-box assessment into individual development plans — with specific commitments, not vague intentions.

- Accountability is a culture, not a monitoring system. Build it by modelling it first, setting clear standards, and addressing misses early and specifically.

- Psychological safety is the operating condition for high performance. Your behaviour — especially under pressure — determines whether it exists.

- Most high performers signal their departure before they announce it. Act on early warning signals, not confirmed ones.

- Know the difference between mentorship and sponsorship. Both matter. Sponsorship changes careers.

Coming Up: *The Conclusion — Day 91 and Beyond. The 90-day guide ends here. The Long Game of Leadership is just beginning.*

DAY 91 AND BEYOND: PLAYING THE LONG GAME

The guide ends here. The work doesn't.

Day 90 is not a finish line. It is the point at which the scaffolding comes down and the structure you've been building is revealed — to your team, to your stakeholders, and to yourself. What you've done in the last 90 days has set the conditions for everything that follows. The foundation is either solid or it isn't. The trust is either there or it needs more work. The team is either beginning to own the outcome or it's still waiting to be told what to do.

Wherever you land on Day 91, the instruction is the same: keep going. Keep developing. Keep listening. Keep getting it wrong and using that information. Keep finding the Unseen Employees. Keep having the difficult conversations early. Keep modelling the accountability you're asking for. Keep showing up as the Turtle — whole, grounded, and genuinely invested in the people you lead.

This is what the Long Game of Leadership looks like. Not a sprint followed by recovery. A consistent, intentional, values-driven practice that compounds over time — in your impact, in your team's performance, in your own sense of purpose as a leader.

The Successful Failure Framework: Your Most Reliable Teacher

You will get things wrong. Some of the decisions you made in the first 90 days will look different to you at Day 180 than they did at the time. Some of the people assessments will need to be revised. Some of the priorities you committed to will shift. Some of the trust you built will be tested.

None of that is failure. All of it is data.

In The Power of Whole Human Leadership, I lay out a four-step approach to failing successfully — a framework I have used in every difficult professional moment of my career, from the Mike wrongful termination situation to the leadership I couldn't save at the company that chose cost theatre over people. The framework is simple. It is not easy. But if you use it consistently, failure stops being something to avoid and starts being something to mine.

The Successful Failure Framework — Your Four-Step Process

Use this framework every time something goes wrong — from a missed deliverable to a failed initiative to a leadership moment you'd do differently. The goal is not to feel bad about it. The goal is to extract every drop of value from it and move forward stronger.

Step	What It Means	Your Reflection Question
1. Acknowledge the good	Recognize what you did well, even in a situation that didn't go as planned. There is almost always something.	*What worked? What did you do right that deserves to be carried forward?*
2. Reflect on the error	Look honestly at where you fell short — not to assign blame, but to understand the root cause with clarity.	*What specifically went wrong, and what was your role in it?*
3. Extract the insight	Derive the specific lesson that will change how you act next time. Not a vague 'I'll do better' — a precise behaviour or decision.	*What will you do differently, specifically, the next time you face a similar situation?*
4. Implement the learning	Put the insight into practice immediately — in the next decision, the next conversation, the next hire.	*Where is the nearest opportunity to apply this learning? When will you do it?*

The leaders who grow most consistently are not the ones who make the fewest mistakes. They are the ones who extract the most learning from each one — and who have the self-awareness and the courage to apply that learning before the next opportunity arrives.

The Long Game Is Not About You

Here is the thing about the Long Game of Leadership that took me a long time to fully understand: it is not primarily about your career. It is not about your title, your compensation, your reputation, or your legacy as you'd like it to be written.

It is about the people you lead.

The measure of a Whole Human Leader — the one that actually matters, the one that endures long after you've moved on to the next role — is not what you built or what you delivered. It is who became more because of how you led them. Roger making partner. Mary finding her voice. David getting the account manager role he wasn't supposed to get on paper. The team member who stayed in the organization because you had one honest conversation with them at the right moment.

Those are the outcomes that define the Long Game. And they don't show up on a P&L.

This is what Whole Human Leadership asks of you — not just competence, not just results, but genuine investment in the growth of the people in your orbit. The Turtle builds a bale. It does not swim alone.

> **The measure of a Whole Human Leader is not what you built. It is who became more because of how you led them.**

Keeping Pace: What the Turtle Knows

Turtles are patient. They are not slow — they are strategic. They set the pace rather than reacting to the pace of everyone around them. They carry their protection with them. They surface when the moment requires it and return to the water when it doesn't. They outlive almost everything in their environment, not through aggression or speed, but through consistency, resilience, and an extraordinary capacity to endure.

That is the leadership model. Not the leader who burns brightest for six months and flames out. The leader who is still there at 18 months, at three years, at a decade — still listening, still developing, still playing the Long Game — is the one who builds something that lasts.

Keeping pace means staying in motion without burning out. It means doing the development work consistently rather than in bursts. It means holding the standard even when it would be easier to let it slip. It means continuing to be the Turtle in the moments when the Iron Maiden would be faster, more efficient, and considerably less vulnerable.

It means being willing to keep getting it right, slowly and deliberately, long after the first 90 days have passed and nobody is watching as closely anymore.

Because the best time to be a Whole Human Leader is not when someone is evaluating you. It's every other time.

Action Planning Page: My Long Game Commitments — Day 91 and Beyond

The 90 days are over. These are the commitments that carry you forward. Be specific. Vague commitments are indistinguishable from good intentions — and good intentions alone don't build legacies.

Area	The Question	My Specific Commitment
Self-Development	*What is the one WHL competency I will develop most deliberately in the next 90 days?*	
My Team	*Who am I sponsoring — not just mentoring — and what will I do this quarter on their behalf?*	
Accountability Culture	*What is the one accountability practice I will implement consistently, starting this week?*	
My Leadership Brand	*How will I make my Why and my values visible to my team and stakeholders in the next 90 days?*	
Psychological Safety	*What is one specific behaviour I will change to strengthen psychological safety on my team?*	
Honest Conversations	*Who needs a direct, honest conversation from me in the next 30 days that I have been avoiding?*	
The Unseen Employees	*Who on my broader team or in my organization am I still not seeing? What will I do about it?*	

A Final Word

I started my first COO role at 24. I had no roadmap, no mentor who had done what I was trying to do, and no guide like this one. I learned everything the hard way — through the mistakes, the difficult people, the situations I wasn't prepared for, and the slow, uncomfortable work of figuring out who I actually was as a leader.

What I know now — and what I wish someone had told me then — is this: the first 90 days are not about proving yourself. They are about earning the right to lead. You earn it through listening before you act, through building trust before you build change, through having the difficult conversations early, and through showing up as a whole human — not the armoured version, not the performance, but the real you, values and all.

The Turtle doesn't arrive fully formed. It develops. It carries its protection with it. It keeps pace. It endures.

I became the Turtle. Who are you becoming?

CONTINUE THE JOURNEY

The Leadership Transition Guide is grounded in two books by Victoria Pelletier, and one that looks at what comes before the role:

The Power of Whole Human Leadership — the definitive guide to the WHL framework: the Iron Maiden, the Turtle, the Unseen Employee, CT + EI, empathy, authenticity, and the Long Game. The full depth of every principle in this guide lives there.

Influence Unleashed: Forging a Lasting Legacy Through Personal Branding — the complete personal brand framework: the Four Elements, the Three Acts of Engagement, your Why, your Identity, your UVP, and your Legacy. With the companion workbook for the exercises that go deeper than this guide can.

Before You Leap: The Leader's Guide to Landing in the RIGHT Place — if you're still deciding on your next role rather than stepping into one, this companion guide and workbook is where to start. The right transition begins long before Day One.

If this guide has been useful and you want to go further — through 1:1 coaching, advisory, or keynote work — visit:

www.victoria-pelletier.com

#Unstoppable | #NoExcuses | #WholeHumanLeadership

VICTORIA PELLETIER

The Turnaround Queen | CEO Whisperer | Whole Human Leader

Victoria Pelletier is a globally recognized executive leader, bestselling author, and keynote speaker with over 30 years of experience leading transformational change across Fortune 500 companies, professional services firms, and technology organizations.

She has held multiple C-suite roles — including COO, President, and CEO — and has navigated more than 100 corporate restructures and 40+ mergers and acquisitions across three continents. It is that track record — not just of delivering results, but of doing it while building cultures people actually want to be part of — that earned her the two nicknames she wears with equal pride: the Turnaround Queen and the CEO Whisperer.

Victoria's leadership philosophy, Whole Human Leadership, is the subject of her book The Power of Whole Human Leadership: Managing Modern Workers Toward Purpose and Profit. It is built on a foundational belief that the most effective leaders are not the ones who leave their humanity at the door — they are the ones who bring all of it, deliberately and consistently, to work. Her second book, Influence Unleashed: Forging a Lasting Legacy Through Personal Branding, extends that philosophy into the realm of personal brand

— laying out a framework for leaders who want to be known not just for what they do, but for who they are.

She is a recognized advocate for diversity, equity, and inclusion, and has received numerous awards for her work advancing women, LGBTQ+ professionals, and underrepresented leaders in the workplace. She is an established keynote speaker whose topics span leadership, resilience, organizational culture, personal branding, and transformation, and whose media appearances include CBC, CNN, and Fox News.

The Leadership Transition Guide is the practical extension of both books — the guide Victoria wishes she had been handed the first time she walked into a new organization as the youngest executive in the building, figuring it out in real time. It is built on everything she has learned since.

ALSO BY VICTORIA PELLETIER

The Power of Whole Human Leadership
Managing Modern Workers Toward Purpose and Profit

Influence Unleashed
Forging a Lasting Legacy Through Personal Branding

Unstoppable
Changemakers Who Dare to Make a Difference

CONNECT WITH VICTORIA

www.victoria-pelletier.com
Keynote speaking |
Executive coaching
Advisory & consulting | 1:1 sessions
linkedin.com/in/victoriapelletier
@victoria_pelletier_unstoppable
#Unstoppable | #NoExcuses

WANT TO GO DEEPER?

This guide is designed to be used independently — but the leaders who move fastest are almost always the ones who have a thinking partner alongside the work. Victoria offers a limited number of 1:1 coaching engagements for senior and mid-level leaders navigating a new role, a post-M&A integration, or a significant leadership transition.

To enquire about availability: **www.victoria-pelletier.com**